I0766533

LETTERS from the FAR LEFT

A Collection of Essays, Articles & Opinions
of a Progressive Dissident

2019

by: J. Thomas Beasley

Published by Kindle Direct Publishing
A DBA of On-Demand Publishing, L.L.C.
An Amazon Company
4900 LaCross Road
North Charleston, SC 29406
USA

March, 2019

Written, edited and prepared for publication by:
J. Thomas Beasley, Esq.
3110 Canal Street
New Orleans, LA 70119

To my wife Happy, who always encourages me to keep talking, even when no one is listening.

FORWARD

Older, wiser, obviously starving for attention, I was determined to share my opinions and knowledge with the world. I already made a living writing legal briefs, and the work was always important – at least to a handful of people. But the prolific writing of memoranda in opposition to motions for summary judgment was not exactly what I envisioned when I dreamt of being a writer as a child. Not that writing "blog" posts on the internet accounting for little more than screaming into the void was precisely my childhood dream either. But it was closer. And it helped to satisfy a nagging itch to exercise my prosaic abilities and to comment on important topics of public debate.

So, for the past few years, I have maintained an online presence, periodically publishing articles and essays on a variety of topics, mostly concerning politics and criminal justice reform – the two areas in which I am most qualified to comment intelligently. Most of the content in this book is still available in various venues online, such as Medium.com and my own personal blog, YourLawScholar.com. The purpose of this publication is to merely aggregate and curate that content for posterity. Or, maybe it is just a vanity project undertaken for my own narcissistic benefit.

Either way the work contained in these pages represents a substantial percentage of my collected efforts of the previous few years, divided loosely into general topics and headings. I hope everyone finds something within that resonates with them, or at least enlightens them, however insignificantly. Joking aside, I am actually not actively pursuing either fame or fortune. I have a day job that I quite appreciate, and continue to perform legal services for disadvantaged clients, and have no immediate plans to discontinue either. Writing is something I do because I enjoy it - it allows my soul to breathe. And if something I write does inspire, elate, enlighten or even mildly interest another person, that would be rewarding enough in itself. But even if no one is touched or moved by my words, that's okay, too. I have dedicated my life to helping people, and will continue to do so whether or not I receive any validation from others. I do what I believe is the right thing to do, because it is the right thing to do.

-J. Thomas Beasley, Esq.

CONTENTS

PREFACE:
A Word About
Truth and Consequence

He walked out onto the sound stage, looking taut, charming, authoritative, dressed in a conservative charcoal (clearly tailored) suit with a light blue shirt, his gold rimmed glasses perched stoically on his nose. He took a seat as the other panelists arrived and the cameras began rolling, sending a live broadcast of Neil out into the universe where an impossible number of people would sit in front of their televisions, hungry to either attack or support Neil's point of view, and Neil never broke a sweat.

Neil Newhouse was the co-founder of Public Opinion Strategies, a national political and public affairs survey research firm. Neil is a Duke-educated professional pollster who has helped countless high-profile candidates get elected, including former Florida governor Jeb Bush, Connecticut Governor John Rowland, Pennsylvania Senator Rick Santorum, Kansas Senator Pat Roberts, and most famously, Massachusetts Governor Mitt Romney. But this wasn't a state gubernatorial election - this time Neil was working on Mr. Romney's (almost successful) presidential campaign.

A few weeks before Neil sat in that ABC studio to discuss the November election, the Romney campaign had rolled out a series of attack ads against incumbent Barrack Obama. The ads accused President Obama of "gut[ting] welfare reform," by removing the work requirement originally put in place under the Clinton administration. Romney himself is seen proclaiming that under Obama's welfare plan, "you wouldn't have to work - they just send you your welfare check." Apparently, according to Romney representatives, the ads were very effective.

Unfortunately for Neil and the Romney campaign, various media outlets, including Politifact.com, researched the changes in the welfare law passed under Obama, and discovered that Romney's claims were either greatly exaggerated, or downright false. What the Obama administration had done was to grant discretionary welfare waivers after governors of multiple states, including Republicans, asked for "more flexibility in how they hand out welfare dollars." In other words, he let the individual states decide how to administer benefits, a historically (and ironically) Republican ideal.

Many of the major news outlets ran with the story, slamming the Romney campaign for making false or misleading claims in campaign ads. Politifact.com, using their clever rating system, rated the welfare ads "Pants on Fire," and the Washington Post playfully taunted by giving the ads "Four Pinocchios." It should have been a blow to the campaign - but it wasn't. It should have at least prompted Romney to pull the ads - but it didn't.

Another Romney campaign strategist, Ashley O'Connor, also present at the ABC panel discussion, lauded the ads, claiming that "[o]ur most effective ad is our welfare ad." When Neil Newhouse was questioned about the false ads, he calmly replied that "[f]act checkers come to this with their own sets of thoughts and beliefs, and we're not going to let our campaign be dictated by fact checkers." He actually said that he wasn't going to let fact-checkers - people who seek to confirm the veracity of statements - affect the Romney campaign's decisions about what information it chose to use.

Thus, the term "fact-checkers" took on a derogatory connotation. Conservative politicians decided, and proclaimed, that verifying facts was a waste of time and had no place in politics, and they went on to demonize those liberal wonks that dared to test the veracity of statements made by conservative pundits and elected officials. The Republican Party, perhaps inadvertently, had just declared a war on facts. And the War wages on.

This was not the first time that someone, or some group, or some organization has attempted to verify and/or falsify statements made by politicians. The Romney campaign was not the genesis of the fact-checking phenomenon. But it did seem to gain some mainstream exposure after that famous quip. Perhaps it is the extreme volume and availability of instant information we have access to today. The internet, 24-hour news stations, social media, smart phones, all the trappings of 21st century life in the developed world, have made it easy for anyone to be an investigative journalist.

Perhaps in the past we had to accept what our leaders told us, unless we were skilled at research, and had time and resources to go out and hunt for information to challenge the narratives of pundits and politicians. Perhaps we only accepted it then, because it was so easy to just let it go. As long as there are no direct consequences to us, why bother? And if we didn't agree with what the guy said, we could call him a liar, or a crook, without the fear of someone else checking OUR facts.

But with the advent of the information age, the magic curtain has been swept aside, and we can see the old fool inside the booth. The days of looking up to our elected leaders as being smarter, more informed, more capable, and armed with more knowledge than the average citizenry are numbered, if not already gone. For many of us, the frustrated minority who actually pay attention, the shine is definitely off the apple. Most of these guys now seem less-informed, more ignorant, than average folks. They tell the same lies, and a detached majority may still believe it, as long as it jibes with their pre-conceived notions, but if you spend a little time listening, you will find it difficult not to smell the bullshit.

I began writing in earnest around the time Barack Obama began his second term as President of the United States. I had been an attorney for several years at the time, and was working for the New Orleans Public Defenders office, representing clients in felony cases. I was, perhaps naively, astonished at the amount of disinformation that was spread by newspapers, and politicians, particularly as it concerned the criminal justice system. I was appalled at the level of deceit engaged in by police officers and prosecutors anxious to get convictions against the poorest members of our society. And there was a constant struggle trying to convince potential jurors of these very real deceptions that they had no doubt been inundated with. But there is only so much you can do as an attorney without running afoul of ethics rules.

So, I wrote. Not as an attorney, but as a member of the general public. Attempting to shed light on uncomfortable truths, and hoping to spark debate on serious public policy issues. The articles that follow are some of my favorites from the past several years that speak to issues I am particularly passionate about. I have always tried to offer a different point of view than the prevailing narrative, and have sought simply to share my own knowledge and experience with others. I have no delusions of changing the world with these writings, but I hope to at least encourage others to question authority, and suspend credulity, at least occasionally. But most importantly, I hope others will follow my lead, and seek knowledge – seek the truth – for no other reason than to be informed in a world of misinformation.

CHAPTER ONE
The First Amendment

"Restriction of free thought and free speech is the most dangerous of all subversions. It is the one un-American act that could most easily defeat us."

- William O. Douglas

I.
A First Amendment Refresher Course for President Trump

Donald Trump, who became President of the United States in an electoral college victory over Hillary Clinton in November 2016, has been branded as perhaps the least qualified president in modern history. He has no prior government experience, and seems to lack even a vague awareness of how our political system functions. But most alarmingly, he seems either completely ignorant of, or completely hostile to the U.S. Constitution. And to think, he has been running for president for well over a year, and has been the president-elect for almost a month, but hasn't taken 15 minutes to even peruse the short, 4-page document that forms the foundation of our democracy. But I know he's been busy. So, I decided to help out a bit, and offer a quick little refresher on some key parts. And we should start with the First Amendment, since it appears to be the one he most often ignores or overlooks.

The First Amendment to the U.S. Constitution is a very busy little paragraph that confers basic human rights on all Americans. Conservatives usually only quote this Amendment when some person tries to claim religious freedom to discriminate against other groups of people. But there is so much more to it than that. The text states, succinctly:

"Congress shall make no law respecting an establishment of religion, or prohibiting the free exercise thereof; or abridging the freedom of speech, or of the press; or the right of the people peaceably to

assemble, and to petition the Government for a redress of grievances."

It seems pretty straightforward, but there is a lot of context in those eloquent few words. While it does grant people the right to the "free exercise" of religion, it also, at least as importantly, prohibits the government from having any dealings with religion. These are two separate clauses, the Free Expression clause, and the Establishment Clause. The Establishment Clause was specifically written to build "a wall of separation between Church & State." See my discussion of this subject in more detail in the next section.

The "Free Exercise" clause does, indeed, prohibit the enacting of any laws that discriminate against a person for practicing their religion. It allows the freedom of people of all different religions to worship as they see fit, so long as their exercise of that right does not infringe upon the rights of others. Because, just as the Free Exercise clause grants people the right to freedom *of* religion, it also extends that right to others' freedom *from* religion. Thus, we don't allow human sacrifices, or honor killings, or forced marriages, or the denying of marriage licenses to people whose "lifestyle" conflicts with someone's religious beliefs. It seems simple enough - you leave me alone to practice whatever religion or lifestyle I choose, and I'll leave you alone to practice whatever religion or lifestyle you choose.

Next we have the Freedom of Speech clause. Now a lot of people - especially our president-elect - have a problem acknowledging this little clause, at least as it concerns speech that is offensive or disagreeable to them. The freedom of speech clause protects the right of citizens to be free from censorship, and to be free to express their ideas, beliefs and opinions in print, media or otherwise publicly, with very limited exceptions. The government maintains the ability to regulate certain speech, such as outlawing "hate speech," or speech that threatens an immediate breach of the peace, or moderating vulgarity and regulating commercial speech. The greatest protections, however, are afforded to speech that is political in nature. Any attempt to restrict the public right to comment on government and politics is subjected to the highest scrutiny by the courts.

In the first half of the 20th century, there were a number of attempts by the government to limit political speech that was critical of the government, or that was "revolutionary." In *Whitney v. California*, for instance, the Supreme Court upheld the arrest and prosecution of a Communist Party organizer for "criminal syndicalism." Justice Brandeis wrote his famous concurring opinion which tacitly introduced the concept of "clear and present danger" into freedom of speech analysis. In essence, while Brandeis concurred with the judgment of the Court, his agreement was based on the application of the Fourteenth Amendment, and he was openly hostile to the opinion of the majority that sought to curtail free speech. In upholding full and free speech, Brandeis stated that while legislatures have a right to curb truly dangerous expression, they must define clearly the nature of that danger. Mere fear of unpopular ideas will not do. He eloquently summarized his opinion thusly:

"Those who won our independence ... believed that freedom to think as you will and to speak as you think are means indispensable to the discovery and spread of political truth; that, without free speech and assembly, discussion would be futile; that, with them, discussion affords ordinarily adequate protection against the dissemination of noxious doctrine; that the greatest menace to freedom is an inert people; that public discussion is a political duty, and that this should be a fundamental principle of the American government ... Recognizing the occasional tyrannies of governing majorities, they amended the Constitution so that free speech and assembly should be guaranteed."

In addition to spoken and written speech, the freedom of speech clause also encompasses the freedom of expression of ideas and opinions through other means of expression. A couple days ago, our new president suggested that people who protest government policies by burning a flag should be imprisoned or have their citizenship stripped. Apparently Mr. Trump does not recall that the U.S. Supreme Court has declared, more than once, that flag-burning is protected speech under the First Amendment. Specifically, in *Texas v. Johnson*, 491 U.S. 397 (1989), the Court struck down all federal and state statutes that proscribed criminal penalties for flag desecration. The following year, the *Johnson* decision was reaffirmed in *U.S. v. Eichman*, 496 U.S. 310 (1990), which struck down a new Flag Protection Act enacted by Congress in response to the *Johnson* decision. Since then, there has been an ongoing effort by conservative lawmakers to enact a Constitutional Amendment abolishing the right to desecrate the American flag, but so far the Amendment has not even received the required Congressional support, let alone the support of 3/4 of State legislatures. So, at least for now, Mr. Trump cannot put people in prison or kick them out of the country for burning a flag, regardless of how offensive such an act may seem.

In addition to these other rights, the First Amendment also confers the right to freedom of the press. Like the freedom of speech, freedom of press is, and should be, a jealously-guarded right of citizens. Nothing keeps the power structure in check better than a robust and unrestricted press. From the landmark decision of *Near v. Minnesota* (1931) which firmly rejected any law that sought to censor publications, also known as "prior restraint", to the case of *Miami Herald v. Tornillo* (1974), which struck down a statute requiring a newspaper to publish a response from any political or public figure that the paper had previously criticized, the Supreme Court has always been openly supportive of a free and unrestrained press.

Here again, we find that president Trump is either ignorant or defiant of First Amendment protections. At one point in his campaign, he suggested that he would "open up libel laws," making it easier to sue members of the press that published negative articles about public figures, and he actually threatened to sue the New York Times for a report in which two women accused Trump of groping them.

"I'm going to open up our libel laws . . .so when they write purposely negative and horrible and false articles, we can sue them and win lots of money."

Apparently he missed the unanimous 1964 Supreme Court decision in *New York Times v Sullivan*, where the court held that any public figure suing for libel must prove that a defamatory statement

23

was made with actual malice, "with knowledge that it was false or with reckless disregard of whether it was false or not." Additionally, he has threatened to "break up" media conglomerates that criticize him, and has been openly hostile to several members of the press, mocking specific reporters as "neurotic," "dumb," and a "waste of time." The Committee to Protect Journalists has declared that Trump is an "unprecedented threat" to free press. And most recently, Trump has tapped conservative talk radio host Laura Ingraham as a potential White House press secretary. Ingraham has displayed severe hostility and disdain towards media, even calling Spanish-speaking news outlets "toxic" and claiming that they "revile the American experience."

Finally, the First Amendment provides Americans with the freedom to peaceful assembly, another stumbling block for president Trump. In *United States v. Cruikshank* (1875), the Supreme Court held that "the right of the people peaceably to assemble for the purpose of petitioning Congress for a redress of grievances, or for anything else connected with the powers or duties of the National Government, is an attribute of national citizenship, and, as such, under protection of, and guaranteed by, the United States. The very idea of a government, republican in form, implies a right on the part of its citizens to meet peaceably for consultation in respect to public affairs and to petition for a redress of grievances."

Trump has frequently lambasted protesters at his rallies, often inciting violence against them from his supporters. In fact on Feb. 1, Trump flat out encouraged it and said he'd cover legal fees if anyone got in trouble for doing what he told them to do.

"If you see somebody getting ready to throw a tomato, knock the crap out of them. Just knock the hell out of them. I promise you, I will pay for the legal fees."

A few weeks later, Trump, speaking about a protester, said to a raucous crowd, "I'd like to punch him in the face" before he began reminiscing about the "old days" where guys like that would be "carried out on a stretcher."

Since his election, he has also criticized protesters, finding that it was "unfair" that American citizens would assemble to voice their opinion of Trump's victory. Sorry, Mr. President, it is not unfair for Americans to exercise their fundamental rights guaranteed by the Constitution.

So there you have it. The president of the United States, who has apparently never read the First Amendment (or any of the Constitution), has an ongoing history of hostility to pretty much every right and privilege conveyed therein. I sincerely hope that people who are smarter than Trump will, at some point, sit down and at least review with him the fundamental rights of Americans guaranteed by this nation's laws. Because Mr. Trump had to raise his right hand and swear to the American people that he will "preserve, protect and defend the Constitution of the United States," his continued ignorance of which guarantees his failure thereto.

II.
Separation of Church and State: America is Not a "Christian Nation"

Most people will recall that in 2018, U.S. immigration authorities, acting at the direction of President Donald Trump, began enacting a policy of separating families of undocumented immigrants at our southern border. Rightfully so, there was a vociferous opposition to this policy, which frequently saw small children taken away from the their parents in held in separate detention facilities alone. At one point in the debate, Attorney General Jefferson Beauregard Sessions, III, sought to justify the separation of migrant children from their migrant families by quoting Paul's letter to the Romans in the New Testament. According to Sessions, the Apostle Paul commanded people "to obey the laws of the government because God has ordained them for the purpose of order . . and lawful processes are good in themselves and protect the weak and lawful." This seems to be another one of those "render unto Cesar that which is Cesar's" lines which the early Christians seemed fond of repeating, but he used it to vouch for a very un-Christian action, because, you know, laws.

It is interesting that the primary counterargument posed by dissenters was to quote other biblical verses in response, pointing out how un-Christian forceful separation of families is, instead of quoting the First Amendment, which might serve to remind Mr. Sessions that preaching by a public official is prohibited. So, instead of pointing out how the bible really says something different than Jeff Sessions says, we should be pointing out that the bible is -or at least should be - *wholly irrelevant* to any dispute we have with our government.

Detractors of this view will invariably insist that we cannot completely divorce our political discourse from biblical notions of morality, suggesting that religion - and in particular Judeo-Christian religion - is the foundation of all modern civilization. They will invoke the old canard that "America is a Christian nation!" This notion has been debunked many times before, but its as if those pious lawmakers weren't listening, or something. America **is not** a Christian nation - it is a secular nation which preserves and supports absolute religious freedom. But virtually nothing that underlies American democracy can be traced back to any Judeo-Christian fundamentals.

America is a nation full of Christians - with approximately 70% of the population professing some level of faith in the doctrine of Christianity. However, that does not mean that America is a Christian Nation. In fact, our founders were quite adamant on this point. Not only did they make an explicit declaration within the body of the U.S. Constitution prohibiting any religious test for public office, the Bill of Rights also contains a 2-part prohibition on the meddling of government in religious matters, what has been described as "excessive entanglements" between government and religion. If their intentions were not clear enough, Thomas Jefferson, one of the principal drafters of our Constitution, wrote a letter in 1802 declaring that "I contemplate with sovereign reverence that act of the whole American people which declared that their legislature should 'make no law respecting an establishment of religion, or prohibiting the free exercise thereof,' *thus building a wall of separation between Church & State.*" And John Adams famously proclaimed that "the Government of the United States of America is not, in any sense, founded on the Christian religion."

It is not difficult to understand why our founding fathers sought to drive a wedge between religion and government. One need only glance at European history, much of it dominated by theocratic rule by the Roman Catholic church, to see why religious tolerance and secularism in politics was so important to our Constitution's framers. Thus, it was an essential feature of our fledgling democracy to keep it safe from the oppression that inevitably accompanies sectarian government.

The "Religious Test" Clause, which is contained in Article VI of the Constitution, states ""no religious Test shall ever be required as a Qualification to any Office or public Trust under the United States." This rather innocuous phrase was designed to keep the government free from undue influence from a religious group. Without such a prohibition, it would be exceedingly easy to exclude certain groups of people from having any voice in the government, and would be a short path to oppression of minorities, such as Jews or Muslims. Unfortunately, while the government cannot impose religious restrictions, in practice our elected officials are oftentimes subject to public requirements of religiosity, at least tacitly. In other words, anyone running for public office who is insufficiently religious is likely doomed to defeat. In fact, in a recent Gallup poll, nearly half (43%) of those polled admitted that they would not vote for an atheist for president.   African-Americans, Women, Jews, Muslims and Homosexuals are all more electable than an atheist, according to the poll. And politicians know this. That's why religion is such an important topic on the campaign trail.

The more ambitious provision in favor of secularism is the Establishment Clause of the First Amendment, which states "Congress shall make no law respecting an establishment of religion, or prohibiting the free exercise thereof..." That short, concise statement is an enormously powerful pronouncement of the founders' secular ideals. It is actually two separate, but equally important, doctrines in one.   The first part essentially prevents the government from making laws specifically in favor of any religion. Justice Hugo Black summed it up thusly:

> The "establishment of religion" clause of the First Amendment means at least this: Neither a state nor the federal government can set up a church. Neither can pass laws which aid one religion, aid all religions, or prefer one religion over another. Neither can force nor influence a person to go to or to remain away from church against his will or force him to profess a belief or disbelief in any religion. No person can be punished for entertaining or professing religious beliefs or disbeliefs, for church attendance or non-attendance. No tax in any amount, large or small, can be levied to support any religious activities or institutions, whatever they may be called,

or whatever form they may adopt to teach or practice religion. Neither a state nor the Federal Government can, openly or secretly, participate in the affairs of any religious organizations or groups and vice versa.

The second part of the clause is known as the "Free Exercise" clause, which prohibits any law that restricts a person's right to practice the religion of his or her choice. Of course there are limitations of things we allow people to do in the name of religion - no human sacrifices, for instance - but otherwise a person's religious preference and their freedom to practice it are sacrosanct. This has always allowed America to be a veritable melting pot of different cultures, ideas and expressions. It allows Catholics, Muslims and Jews to co-exist peacefully alongside a multitude of other various faiths as well as the faith-less. It is the hallmark of America's heritage of tolerance, and should be jealously guarded.

What I find disturbing, given the history of our religious freedom, is the rhetoric of the conservative politicians who frequently cite the Bible, God, religion, Christianity or some other religious source as the motivation and/or justification for public policy. And I would hope that reasonable Americans, even ones that are devoutly religious, would find it disturbing as well. Allowing our leaders and lawmakers to invoke divine providence in their decision-making process is a dangerous proposition. Not only does it run the risk of Biblical doctrine supplanting our "earthly" laws, it is also exclusionary to anyone who doesn't believe in the same God. In other words, if the president says Jesus told him to act in a certain way, then anyone who isn't Christian is going to be excluded from that conversation. At present, at least 30% of the U.S. population identifies as something other than Christian. To invoke Christianity in public policy is to disenfranchise nearly a third of the population.

Even if 99% of the US population was Christian, invoking Christianity in public discourse, and describing our nation as a Christian Nation, is still insensitive and contrary to the principals our nation was founded upon. The Bill of Rights, and all other civil liberties that have been endowed upon Americans throughout our history, provide fundamental rights to everyone. These enumerated rights and liberties have been set forth precisely to protect those in the minority. The majority needs no special protection from encroachment upon their rights - they are in the majority! It is another hallmark of our democracy that everyone, including those in the minority, are equal under the law.

Yet here we are, in 2018, listening to highly educated men and women invoking faith to justify laws that allow people to discriminate against homosexuals; to block women's access to birth control and abortion; and to mandate the teaching of "creationism" from the Book of Genesis in public school science classes. We see Republican candidates having arguments over who is the more devout Christian. And we have conservative lawmakers proclaiming that God and the Bible are the sources that guide their decision-making, instead of the Constitution and the laws of the United States of America. This is troubling, at the very least. Politicians rail against oppressive regimes in the Muslim world that practice Sharia Law, yet if they were given their way they would undoubtedly install a version of Sharia, based on the Christian bible, here in America. We must be vigilant against any such attempt, lest we regress to a time when "sins" were defined by the church, and punished cruelly. We owe it to our ancestors, and our progeny, to protect our sacred tradition of separation of church and state, which is a fundamental component of a successful democracy, where everyone, religious and impious, Baptist and Mormon, Muslim and atheist all have the same rights, freedoms and liberties. America is filled with Christians, but America is NOT a Christian. America is a democratic republic, a paragon of progress and inclusion, defined by personal and individual freedom, and it is blind to race, color, sexual preference and religion. America is a Secular Nation, which is the *only* option if we intend to keep our place as one of the greatest nations in the history of civilization.

III.
The Uncertain Intersection Between Free Speech and Social Media

In the late summer of 2018, a war of words erupted amongst the populace over the de-platforming of one or more outspoken public figures, including the irascible Alex Jones. Social media sites, such as Facebook and YouTube banned Alex Jones' content for violation of various terms of service ("ToS"). The public outcry was, frankly, rather surprising. Although I fully expected Jones' right-wing audience to have apoplectic fits of rage, there was an almost equally vocal contingent of left-leaning personalities objecting to the public shaming of a thoroughly heinous conservative idealogue. And the argument on both sides seems to focus on the same thing - the dangers of censorship and the inevitable erosion of our freedom of speech.

I tend to agree with the general sentiment. I am a First Amendment absolutist, and believe that any censorship - even of vile ideas - is a violation of the most fundamental right we can have as a free society. However, I stand in a unique position amongst my fellow citizens, in that while I express disdain for the impulse to silence unpopular speech, I also believe that this particular hill is not one I am willing to die upon. Because, like it or not, this was not a violation of the First Amendment. So while my gut instinct is to recoil at the thought of silencing speech, the fact of the matter is that the First Amendment does not protect citizens from *private* actions.

The First Amendment to the U.S. Constitution is a very busy little paragraph that confers basic human rights on all Americans. Conservatives usually only quote this Amendment when some person tries to claim religious freedom to discriminate against other groups of people - you know, its their protection from "the gays." But there is so much more to it than that. The text states, succinctly:

"Congress shall make no law respecting an establishment of religion, or prohibiting the free exercise thereof; or abridging the freedom of speech, or of the press; or the right of the people peaceably to assemble, and to petition the Government for a redress of grievances."

In that short and loaded passage, we find the Freedom of Speech clause - barely six words long, yet spawning hundreds of thousands of words interpreting, defining and applying it. For centuries, Americans have had trouble processing this clause, particularly when it concerns speech that is offensive or disagreeable to them. But in a nutshell, the freedom of speech clause protects the right of citizens to be free from *government* censorship, and to be free to express their ideas, beliefs and opinions in print, media or otherwise publicly, with very limited exceptions. And this means that the *government* cannot make laws that prohibit a person, or group, or company from speaking publicly concerning just about any subject.

However, the government does maintain the ability to regulate certain speech, such as outlawing "hate speech," or speech that threatens an immediate breach of the peace, or moderating vulgarity and regulating commercial speech. Various Supreme Court decisions have carved out narrow exceptions to protect society from particularly dangerous or obscene speech. It's why you don't hear "fuck" on network television, for example. It's why there are laws against yelling "Fire" in a crowded theater. Certain speech has been deemed to possess the ability to cause immediate danger to citizens, and therefore there simply must be some common-sense regulation.

The greatest protections, however, are afforded to speech that is political in nature. Any attempt to restrict the public right to comment on government and politics is subjected to the highest scrutiny by the courts. In the first half of the 20th century, there were a number of attempts by the government to limit political speech that was critical of the government, or that was "revolutionary." In *Whitney v. California*, for instance, the Supreme Court upheld the arrest and prosecution of a Communist Party organizer for "criminal syndicalism." Justice Brandeis wrote his famous concurring opinion which tacitly introduced the concept of "clear and present danger" into freedom of speech analysis. In essence, while Brandeis concurred with the judgment of the Court, his agreement was based on the application of the Fourteenth Amendment, and he was openly hostile to the opinion of the majority that sought to curtail free speech. In upholding full and free speech, Brandeis stated that while legislatures have a right to curb truly dangerous expression, they must define clearly the nature of that danger. Mere fear of unpopular ideas will not do. He eloquently summarized his opinion thusly:

"Those who won our independence ... believed that freedom to think as you will and to speak as you think are means indispensable to the discovery and spread of political truth; that, without free speech and assembly, discussion would be futile; that, with them, discussion affords ordinarily adequate protection against the dissemination of noxious doctrine; that the greatest menace to freedom is an inert people; that public discussion is a political duty, and that this should be a fundamental principle of the American government ... Recognizing the occasional tyrannies of governing majorities, they amended the Constitution so that free speech and assembly should be guaranteed."

And it can be fairly argued that Alex Jones' speech was primarily political in nature, although he frequently segued into laughable conspiracy theories that seem unconnected to anything in this reality. He was a vocal supporter of Donald Trump, and a vicious opponent of Democrats, often using hateful rhetoric to drive his point home. Among his "political" views, he espoused disgusting theories about the 9/11 terror attacks, and perhaps most heinously, he attacked survivors of the Sandy Hook school shooting, insisting that the entire event was staged. He went so far as to publish home addresses of survivors and victims' families, with the unfortunate result that several of these people were harassed by a few of Jones' more idiotic fans. In fact, it could be argued that some of the speech engaged in by Jones was potentially illegal, including hate speech and defamation. He even encouraged people, at least tacitly, to set transgender people on fire, which could be prosecuted as an incitement to violence. So, just at a first blush, there was much that Jones said that could and should be outlawed, even under a liberal application of the First Amendment.

But that's not even what happened. As of the time of this writing, I am unaware of any governmental action taken to silence Jones, or any other controversial pundit. What happened is that YouTube, Facebook and Apple chose to discontinue support for any of his content. These are all private corporations, and they all cited violations of their respective terms of service in support of their business decision to de-platform this madman. Perhaps if there was some discriminatory intent, which may run afoul of Equal Protection rights, there would be a valid grievance against these decisions. But again, as far as I can tell, Alex Jones was not booted for his inclusion in a 'protected class' of citizens, but because his brand of toxic hatecraft was bad for business for these companies. The same reason ABC cancelled Roseanne after her Ambien-fueled racism threatened its sponsors' bottom line, and James Gunn was fired by Disney for tasteless jokes that may have cut into their profits. These were all business decisions, most of which I don't support, but which aren't themselves constitutional violations.

Now, all that said, I am not happy with the power these companies have over content publication. It is a dark feature of America's unique form of absolutist capitalism that allows a few massive corporations to exercise so much power over the American people. By continuing to swallow the capitalist propaganda being spoon-fed to us by the wealthy and their enablers, we have loosened our anti-trust laws, eroded corporate accountability and succumbed to a marketplace that is dominated by corporate rule. Do we need to have a serious discussion about the ability of companies like Facebook and YouTube to dictate what ideas we have access to? Absolutely, probably more than anything. But that is not the conversation that is happening. If there is a movement to create publicly-owned channels of communication and media, I will be first in line to sign up. But as it stands, we aren't having that conversation. And this should be particularly obvious - and hopefully painful - to all the conservative, libertarian free-market cheerleaders out there. This is what you wanted - corporate decisions free from governmental oversight. This is what happens when you privatize the public space. Unless you people agree that private companies shouldn't have this kind of power, then I suggest you suck it up and take what your CEO's of freedom decide to give you.

This is not a victory celebration for anybody. Nobody should be applauding the silencing of a dissident, even one as disgusting as Alex Jones. Anyone who follows progressive thinkers on social media already knows, firsthand, that our views are frequently censored also. And I fear it is going to get worse if we don't come together to address the real problem. If we continue to allow private industry to control all of the mass media outlets free from public oversight, we can expect to see a lot more censorship in the future. And maybe this de-platforming of a right-wing lunatic will be the impetus we need to forge bi-partisan support for breaking up the media monopolies. Until that happens though, I will not defend Alex Jones or his conservative audience. As far as I'm concerned, this is karmic retribution. If you continue to advocate for the private ownership of every aspect of life, eventually your life, thoughts and ideas will be owned as well.

IV.
The Lingering Menace of "Russiagate" and its Potential for Undermining Our First Amendment Rights

On November 8, 2016, Americans cast their vote for the 45th President of the United States, and - somehow - elected Donald J. Trump. Trump defeated Hillary Clinton in the general election, receiving 306 electoral college votes to Hillary's 237. A decisive electoral college victory (yes, I know Clinton won the popular vote, but that is a subject for another day). Few expected Trump to win, with his comically obnoxious behavior and unprecedented ignorance. Most polls taken prior to the election gave Clinton a wide advantage, and the mainstream media all but declared her victory leading up to the election. But, by about 9:00 p.m. or so on November 8, it became shockingly clear that an anti-intellectual reality television star was going to be America's next President. How could this happen?

Of course there are a lot of reasons Trump beat one of the most groomed candidates in the history of presidential politics. Racism, xenophobia and homophobia, along with an unlikely strain of religious fundamentalism, all seemed to lend support to Trump. But there were also economic issues and an eroded public trust in politics - or more specifically, in politicians - and Hillary Clinton was a perfect microcosm of all those things that cause an eroded public trust in politics. And then there was Wikileaks, James Comey, and Russian interference in the election. If you listen to the die-hard Democrats, these last three things were the only reasons Clinton lost - the election was stolen by Kremlin interference orchestrated by Vladimir Putin and FBI Director James Comey.

We are now more than 2 years past the election, and U.S. Intelligence agencies have spent hundreds of hours and millions of dollars investigating whether Russian interference influenced the outcome of the 2016 election. It is alleged, although no hard evidence has been made public, that Russian agents were responsible for hacking the Democratic National Committee's servers, stealing emails and other confidential communications that would later be made public by Wikileaks. It is perhaps more clear that Russian agents may have engaged in targeted online propaganda during the campaign, although it is entirely unclear whether those agents were acting at the direction of government officials.

We have a special prosecutor, Robert Mueller, who was appointed to investigate collusion between Russian agents and Trump campaign officials. So far, Mueller has handed down indictments against several of Trump's campaign staff, including Paul Manafort and Michael Flynn, but it is important to note that none of these indictments include allegations of conspiracy or collusion with Russia regarding the 2016 election. We may or may not see such allegations in the future.

There may be something to the Russiagate allegations. There are some who believe the entire "scandal" is a baseless conspiracy theory, but I'm not totally convinced. There may be something there. And if there is evidence that Russia violated international law and unlawfully interfered in our elections, we should be outraged and Russia should be sanctioned. And if our President's campaign deliberately colluded with Russia to unlawfully interfere in our elections, they should be removed and prosecuted. But as it stands, the worst "crime" alleged against Russia is that they spread gossip on Facebook aimed at discrediting Hillary Clinton - an endeavor that is not extraordinarily difficult to undertake.

"Fake news" - the most popular phrase of the Trump presidency - is the real culprit (according to party-loyal Democrats) behind Hillary Clinton's historic loss. The Russian propaganda was "fake news" that was deliberately spread on Facebook and the internet to discredit Clinton in an effort to influence people to vote for Donald Trump. Fake news caused so many Americans to abandon Clinton in favor of the most unpopular presidential candidate in modern history that it caused perhaps the biggest upset in modern presidential election history. And Trump, the most unpopular presidential candidate in modern history, has hijacked this idea - even going so far as taking credit for inventing the word "fake" - and accused all of the mainstream media, with the possible exception of Fox News, of spreading disinformation. Every negative word ever said about Trump is "Fake News!" according to him. And this is where it starts to get a little scary.

Even before Trump took office, while Obama was winding down his last weeks as President, he signed a law authorizing an executive branch committee "to counter active measures by the Russian Federation to exert covert influence over peoples and governments." Additionally, in a separate but related

43

bill, an inter-agency body would be created to develop "procedures to expose and refute foreign misinformation and disinformation and proactively promote fact-based narratives and policies to audiences outside the United States." Ostensibly, these provisions are designed to simply "expose and refute" disinformation and propaganda from *foreign* sources, but let's be honest - government agencies have been known on occasion to expand their reach far beyond their originally-intended scope. So, this executive body could effectively allow for the creation of a frighteningly-Orwellian Ministry of Truth, blocking all unapproved messages, and putting forth factual information as determined by un-elected bureaucrats. This should be cause for concern.

Additionally, just this week we saw French President Emmanuel Macron introduce legislation intended to end the spread of disinformation on social media and online. The bill would allow judges to block a website or user account if it is determined - by the government - that they are publishing disinformation. Enforcement would be particularly strict during elections. The law has, understandably, generated a significant degree of opposition, but with a solid majority in parliament, Macron still has a good chance of getting it passed. This is exactly the type of response we should be worrying about.

Which brings us to the thesis of this piece. If Russia had anything to do with "hacking the election," the purpose behind it would almost have to have been to undermine our democracy. And the reaction by Americans - mostly Democrats and Trump-haters - to this perceived wrongdoing by Russia may very well lead to a massive undermining of our democracy. The solution to securing the American people from foreign propaganda and "disinformation" can be combated by creating a governmental agency tasked with censoring content and creating and publishing counter-narrative content of its own. In essence, the humble beginnings of an authoritarian police state.

What should be even scarier than that - lest someone accuse me of being pro-Trump - is that Trump is a maniac, and, at the time of this writing, is currently the Chief Executive Officer of the United States government. That means that an uninformed, prejudiced, and massively untruthful imbecile could be the first to oversee the curation and dissemination of government-approved media content. Trump's behavior and attitude have frequently resembled the machinations of authoritarian leaders, and his insistence that all of this nation's most respected news and media outlets publish nothing but fake news bodes ill for how such a power might be wielded.

The First Amendment to the U.S. Constitution guarantees freedom of speech and the press, each of which has been described as a "fundamental personal right." Nothing keeps the power structure in check better than a robust and unrestricted press. From the landmark decision of *Near v. Minnesota* (1931) which firmly rejected any law that sought to censor publications, also known as "prior restraint", to the case of *Miami Herald v. Tornillo* (1974), which struck down a statute requiring a newspaper to publish a response from any political or public figure that the paper had previously criticized, the Supreme Court has always been openly supportive of a free and unrestrained press. The freedoms guaranteed in the First Amendment are crucial to the functioning of our democracy, as stated eloquently by Justice Brandeis in the landmark case of *Whitney v. California*:

"Those who won our independence ... believed that freedom to think as you will and to speak as you think are means indispensable to the discovery and spread of political truth; that, without free speech and assembly, discussion would be futile; that, with them, discussion affords ordinarily adequate protection against the dissemination of noxious doctrine; that the greatest menace to freedom is an inert people; that public discussion is a political duty, and that this should be a fundamental principle of the American government ... Recognizing the occasional tyrannies of governing majorities, they amended the Constitution so that free speech and assembly should be guaranteed."

This goes beyond party lines. Whether you are a liberal, conservative, libertarian or anarchist, you should be concerned about the consequences - both intended and unintended - of following Russiagate too far down the rabbit hole. We may find out that the "solution" to Russian interference is to cede our freedom of press (and speech) to the executive branch, and whichever lunatic happens to be its current leader. Unless you found yourself cheering for O'Brian while he tortured Winston Smith in Orlwell's classic 1984, you should be uncomfortable with the idea of our own government exercising control over what ideas to which Americans will be allowed exposure. By making Russiagate into a bogeyman that must be fought at all costs, combined with our President's open hostility to negative news, I fear a new era of authoritarian censorship may be on the horizon.

CHAPTER TWO
Presidential Aspirations

"A presidential campaign may easily degenerate into a mere personal contest, and so lose its real dignity. There is no indispensable man."

\- Woodrow Wilson

V.
Disrespecting The President

In January, 2017, Barack Obama ended his eight year residence as the 44th President of the United States. Donald Trump had somehow won the election, and Republicans were handed, however briefly, total control of the U.S. government. And in the midst of this blossoming administration, Republicans complained of all the negativity they received from Democrats and the media. They demanded we have respect for President Trump – it wasn't dignified to insult and criticize sitting Presidents and the distinguished gentlemen of Congress. Apparently, the entire G.O.P. was struck with amnesia, completely forgetting how much "respect" they showed Obama for eight years.

Recall that little Kenyan boy from Hawaii that became President of the United States. This Kenyan boy Graduated from Columbia University, earned a law degree from Harvard Law School, practiced as a civil rights attorney and was a law professor at University of Chicago Law School. He then served three terms in the Illinois Senate before being elected to the United States Senate in 2004. He had the perfect resume for the job of President when he was elected in 2008. Yet following his inauguration as this nation's 44th President, he became one of the most disrespected people in America - and by far the most disrespected president - ever.

Remember when President Obama was

delivering a nationally televised speech to Congress a mere 8 1/2 months into his first term, and South Carolina representative, Joe Wilson, shouted out "You Lie!" on live television? How petty and childish it is to literally heckle a sitting president as he addresses the nation. What horrible things had he done, less than 9 months into his first term, to earn such blatant and callous disrespect?

Or what about when Jan Brewer, the Governor of Arizona, met with President Obama on the tarmac, and, again on national television, had a heated debate with him about an insult she had lodged against the president in her book. Not only did she "get in Obama's face," at least metaphorically, she actually stuck her finger in his face while yelling at him. I get that she may have been mildly miffed, but this outwardly aggressive encounter didn't need to take place at that moment, in that place, and in that way. It was clearly intentionally orchestrated to convey the utmost disrespect. To top it all off, she responded to criticism by suggesting that she "felt threatened" by the president.

Not long after, when Republicans regained control of Congress, Mitch McConnell (R)(Ky.), specifically stated that "my number one priority is making sure president Obama's a one-term president." He actually said that. In the midst of a financial meltdown, skyrocketing oil prices, terrorism in the middle east, and impending global catastrophe from climate change, the Congressional leadership put "intentionally obstructing the president" as the single most important issue for Congress to address. Whether Mr. McConnell was serious or just being glib doesn't matter - the message was that Republicans had a deep dislike of Barack Obama and would do everything in their power to undermine his authority.

Because that's what it was really about. It's not about how much they disagree with his policies (although they definitely DO disagree with ALL of his policies), or how left-wing-liberal-Democrat-Communist he is (although they DO think he's a left-wing-liberal-Democrat-Communist), but it is really about refusing to accept his legitimacy. Republican politicians and pundits have had an incredibly difficult time acknowledging that Barack Obama is actually the President of the United States.

There were the State of the Union addresses when congressional Republicans rarely, if ever, applauded Obama's victories, and sat stone-faced (I'm looking at you John Boehner and Paul Ryan) as the president laid out the accomplishments of the previous year. Yet, when Obama proclaimed, at his 2015 speech, "I have no more campaigns to run," he was rudely interrupted by a burst of applause by those same Republicans. Of course, Obama retorted with the brilliant but stinging "I know because I won both of them," for which Republicans astonishingly accused the president of being "rude." Is it rude to respond to hecklers? Perhaps. But when its the very same people complaining about the rudeness as were engaging in the undeniably rude heckling in the first place, it sort of smacks of hypocrisy. Republicans are always right, and Obama was always wrong - period.

Don't forget about the "birther" movement, claiming that Obama was not American -that he was actually born in Kenya, and his birth certificate from Hawaii was forged. Or the constant insistence that Obama is actually a Muslim, despite his clear and unambiguous relationship with Christianity. Or the attempt to label him as a "communist," although many of his policies are more to the right of Eisenhower, including his bail-out for banks, the auto industry, and the pushing through of his signature Trans-Pacific Partnership - all pro-business, right-of-center endeavors. And while occasionally being referred to as a monkey, or ape, or other racially incendiary comparison to lower level primates, Republicans have taken to referring to Obama almost ceaselessly as a "community organizer" - like its a bad thing. One can almost hear the "N" word just beneath the surface of that pejorative. The point is, that all of these labels, and all the disrespect that has been bestowed upon our first African-American president, seem to be designed to delineate Obama as something "other." His "otherness" makes him different than past presidents, and not worthy of the respect and esteem that usually accompanies the highest office in the land. I wonder what could be so different about Obama? His education? His political experience? His uncanny acumen for debate and oration? No, I think it's something else...

And, Marco Rubio, who at the time was fighting for third place in the Republican primaries, was upset about a campaign ad by other Republican nominee hopeful (and silent film villain) Ted Cruz. In the ad, Cruz accused Rubio of cooperating with the Obama administration in voting in favor of the Trans-Pacific Partnership. That part was true, as many other Republicans also voted in favor of the TPP, which was generally seen as pro-business, and Rubio did not complain about the underlying message. However, what Rubio resented is that Ted Cruz's campaign photoshopped an image to make it look like Rubio was smiling and shaking the president's hand. Rubio was incensed that Cruz would be so "deceitful" as to make it appear that Rubio actually shook the president's hand. Nothing could be worse to a Republican presidential hopeful than to be viewed as being polite and amiable toward president Obama.

Let me make it clear that I am not an obedient cheerleader with unquestioning allegiance to Barack Obama. While I did vote for him in 2008 and 2012, he was not my first choice. I view many of his policies and positions as antithetical to real liberal values, especially on issues of foreign interventionism and pro-corporate policies. He has signed more death warrants than any other president, and has doubled down on over-reaching spying programs and drone strikes. He has brokered bailouts for Wall Street and the TPP which was likely to lead to even more U.S. manufacturing jobs being outsourced to other countries. His signature legislation, the **PPACA**, is a carbon copy of earlier Republican health care plans that rewards large insurance companies at the expense of the middle class.

However, all these disagreements aside, I have an immense degree of respect for the president. He has done a remarkable job with the terrible mess he inherited. He has reduced the federal budget deficit (which is different than the national debt); he has stewarded a miraculous recovery following near-economic collapse; and he has provided health insurance to millions of Americans that didn't have it before. We have seen an unprecedented expansion of LGBT rights, the beginnings of criminal justice reform and decriminalization of marijuana, as well as sorely-needed gun control measures under his leadership. So, while we may disagree on several fundamental ideological issues, I would never mock, heckle or outright disrespect President Obama. It's about time the rudeness and incivility from impertinent Republicans stops. The American people, by a wide margin, elected a black man president - twice. Sorry if that incenses the right-wing - get over it. He has done a yeoman's job given his inherited circumstances, and he has handled his position (and the constant challenges to his legitimacy) with grace and professionalism. Which is more than I can say for his impudent detractors.

VI.
Presidential Election 2016:
The Growing Discontent

Donald Trump was elected president in November, 2016, in an unexpected upset over Hillary Clinton. I won't delve into too much detail about the Donald at this point, but suffice it to say that his brand of anti-establishment, self-funded, narcissistic self-aggrandizement appears to have resonated with a large fraction of the Republican party – and of the United States. He successfully sold a xenophobic, fear-based political incorrectness to a certain group of core supporters, so much so that no amount of negative press was able to deter his march toward victory.

Hillary Clinton seemed guaranteed to win the election. Most of the major polls leading up to the election gave her a wide margin of victory over Trump. This was supposed to be Hillary's show. She was seen as the only potential candidate to ensure another Democratic president in the White House.

However, she was an avowed establishment politician, and an unabashed war-hawk. As a Senator, she voted in favor of the Iraq War. As Secretary of State, she was instrumental in the decision to bomb Libya, and was complicit in the Honduran coup, both of which have turned out to have nightmarish consequences in those regions. She also comes with a lot of baggage, from Benghazi, to her personal email server, to her unholy alliance with Wall Street and big business (she was once a board member for Wal-Mart and regularly takes large speaking fees from Wall

Street elites). In fact, if you take out her policy positions on women's rights and LGBT equality (something she only recently "evolved" on), she was more closely aligned with centrist Republicans than she was with liberal Democrats.

Because of her baggage, she was challenged for the nomination by the ne'er do well populist from Vermont, Bernie Sanders. Before the 2015 election cycle began, outside of his home state of Vermont, only a handful of policy wonks and news junkies had ever heard of this crazy-haired, bombastic socialist from New England. When he first entered the presidential race, he was literally dismissed as an old, cranky extremist that would never even register with voters. However, ever since, he has built a miraculous new movement in the Democratic party. His "socialist" views are seen as harkening back to the trust-busting days of Teddy Roosevelt, the New Deal policies of Franklin Roosevelt, and the progressive taxation of Dwight Eisenhower. He supports single-payer, Medicare for all type healthcare, taking inspiration from Canada, Australia, and most other developed nations around the world. He has decried the widening gap between the very rich and everyone else, which has also eroded America's once coveted middle class, almost to the point of extinction. And he has made a strong case for removing big money from the political process, and advocates for the reversal of the Supreme Court's *Citizens' United* decision that bestowed First Amendment rights upon large corporations, allowing the wealthiest Americans to donate obscene amounts of money to political candidates. In fact, in building this revolution, Bernie Sanders has refused to take any money from wealthy donors, and has financed his campaigns with millions of small, individual donations. Because of his frank disapproval of status quo politics, and his strong populist message (and nearly pristine record of fighting for equality), Bernie Sanders won a substantial percentage of state primaries in 2016 (including one of the largest upsets in history with his win in Michigan last month), and in the years following, remained one of the most popular politicians in the world, with the highest approval rating of any American politician.

The 2016 election season promised to be a walk in the park for two credentialed, establishment politicians. Democrats were looking to continue "business as usual" in Washington, extending the policies of President Obama, while Republicans looked to capitalize on their big Congressional gains with a candidate that would appeal to their base of anti-government, pro-business supporters. But both sides fell under attack from a growing mass of voters that are simply fed up with the status quo. On the Republican side, a boorish, conceited blowhard continue to rally legions of low-information voters that are tired of political correctness and political double-speak. On the Democratic side, an ornery old hippie has risen to challenge the party's continued rightward movement toward conservatism that rewards big corporate donors while effectively eliminating the middle class. In both cases, what we are seeing is a population of citizens that are finished with establishment politics.

As an example of how little our elected officials listen to voters, there was a study done by Princeton University recently that showed some alarming trends. Their study comprised data from 2000 public opinion surveys and compared the numbers to policies that became law. In other words, they compared what the pubic wanted to what the government actually did. The result was that the opinions of 90% of Americans have **NO IMPACT**. The study suggests that the number of Americans for or against any policy has a "miniscule, near-zero, statistically non-significant impact upon public policy." But monied interests - that other 10% - matters a lot. In a five year period, 200 of the most politically active companies spent about $6 billion on lobbying and campaign contributions. Those same companies received over $4 trillion (with a "T") in taxpayer support. And this is the system that the party elites want to maintain. This is the status quo that is so important to the party leadership, because it is what bankrolls their campaigns, and lines their own pockets.

I agree with the growing dismay of former party loyalists that things need to change in politics. I agree that there is way too much corporate influence in Washington. I agree that we must do something to address the ever-widening wealth gap, when the top 400 wealthiest Americans have more than the bottom 150 million Americans combined. We must stop the relentless profiteering by pharmaceutical companies and hospitals that have made the American healthcare system one of the most expensive in the world. And we must make sure that everyone has a voice, and everyone, regardless of race, religion, or sexual identity, enjoy the same rights as everyone else. These are the things that the Democratic Party used to stand for. It was the party of progressive liberals, seeking to make the world a better place through positive change and social equality. It is the party that brought us Medicare, Social Security, and the Civil Rights Act.

These are the reasons I became a Democrat when I reached voting age more than two decades ago. But the Democratic Party, post-Bill Clinton, has been growing more and more conservative, doubling down on a failed War on Drugs, being complicit in the unjustified war in Iraq, complicit in the adoption of the Patriot Act, one of the most vile affronts to Constitutional principles since Jim Crow, and they have become just as war-ready as the most hawkish Republicans. So, I no longer identify as a party-loyal Democrat. And I know quite a few others that are in the same position.

So what's this mean for the future of American politics? Well, if we listen to our establishment politicians, we have to take small, calculated, politically expedient steps to gradually change... No, that's just politispeak for we must change nothing, and maintain the status quo. What we need is a revolution. We need the people, the citizens, to unite behind a common goal of changing our political system. We may not be able to easily, or even feasibly, dismantle the two-party system in this country, but we can at least demand that the parties once again represent the values of its current and former members. We need to shout to make our voices heard and tell Washington that it is time for the government to work for all Americas, not just the wealthy elite. It's time to end the era of establishment politics financed by billionaires and beholden to special interests.

There is only one person that we can trust to lead our nation toward the brighter tomorrow we have been promised for so long. Bernie Sanders has been a real, American progressive his entire life. He marched on Washington with Martin Luther King, and was arrested alongside African American activists protesting segregation in Chicago. He has been a fearless voice for the equal treatment of the LGBT community for decades, and was an early supporter of marriage equality. He is against fracking, and was against the Keystone XL pipeline, and has recognized that climate change is among the most important threats we face. He voted against the Iraq War; he voted against the Wall Street bailout; he voted against dismantling Glass-Steagle (which precipitated the collapse of the banking system); and he has campaigned on common sense strategies to restore America's middle class, to end corruption in politics, and to make healthcare and education accessible to every single American. Bernie Sanders' rise is a harbinger of the fall of the establishment. He is the future of progressive change. And if the Democratic Party will get its hands out of the pockets of billionaires and re-align with these fundamental principles, I may once again be proud to call myself a Democrat.

VII.
Bernie Sanders' Revolution: The Overton Window and the Populist Left

Bernie Sanders was cheated in 2016. I don't mean to suggest that I know he would have won the nomination if not for cheating, but there is no doubt that he was cheated. The DNC has practically admitted that it purposely shut Sanders out. Superdelegates - unelected party insiders - flat out ignored voters in supporting Clinton, even in states that overwhelmingly supported Sanders. For example, in Washington and Colorado, where Sanders won the primary by a substantial margin, he received the support of ZERO superdelegates. In fact Sanders won at least 45% of the popular vote in the primaries, but only received about 7% of the superdelegates. Then there was the resignation of Debbie Wasserman-Schultz, who was forced to resign amid allegations of bias in the primary. And her successor, Donna Brazile, actually leaked debate questions to Clinton. Not to mention the secret "deal" Clinton made with the DNC to finance the DNC in exchange for almost total party control.

Additionally, there were numerous disturbing allegations of election fraud, voter suppression, and other "irregularities" in state primaries. Such as the purging of 125,000 Democrats from the voting rolls in Sanders' hometown of Brooklyn just before the primary. Or the thousands of voters whose party affiliation was mysteriously switched. Or the massive and unprecedented disparity between exit polls and election results in numerous contests. Or the decision in several states to close a majority of polling places, causing huge lines and ridiculously long waits in order for people to vote. Or the numerous instances of polling places running out of ballots. Or allegations that auditors improperly changed individual votes to cover up discrepancies.

But even absent actual cheating, the primary system itself is flawed, and fails to reflect the will of the actual voters. In numerous states, including New York, Maryland and Pennsylvania, closed primaries prohibited independent voters from voting. Since approximately 45% of voters in the U.S. are declared 'independents,' and Bernie Sanders does far and away better with independents than Mrs. Clinton, her victories in those closed primary states were, at the very least, misleading. There were literally millions of voters that were not able to voice their opinion due to these closed contests. And in the caucus states, which Sanders won overwhelmingly, there is no actual count of the number of votes cast, which makes Clinton's declared margin of victory less than accurate, as well.

Alas, Clinton "won" the Democratic primary in 2016. And somehow, one of the most "qualified" and well-known candidates in history, lost the general election to one of the most unqualified and least-favorable candidates in history. Why? Because she was a terrible candidate. Because she is a relic of the past. Clinton is a "New Democrat," a founding member of the Third Way democrats that have gradually taken over the establishment in the past 3 decades. These Democrats are nothing more than 1980's Republicans, rebranded as the opposition to the New Republicans, which are more akin to 1930's fascist European parties than to the Eisenhower moderates of the 1950's. Today's Democratic party is corrupt in the same way that the Republican party is - they take massive amounts of money from the super-rich and powerful, and return political favors to benefit those super-wealthy donors. Just like the Republicans. In fact, there is practically no difference in the donor lists for the two major parties. And their policies are likewise practically identical, benefiting a handful of wealthy elites, and screwing the middle and working class.

There is a concept in political science known as the "Overton Window." It is a theoretical range of ideas tolerated in public discourse. Essentially, it is a bracket of views and policy proposals that are deemed mainstream, and within which politicians are able to offer promises without fear of being labeled an extremist. Ideally, the political spectrum represents ideas that are considered communist on the extreme left to fascist on the extreme right. In America's heyday, the Overton Window was centered on the center line between these two extremes. Thus, strong Democrats like Franklin D. Roosevelt, could push policies that were substantially left-leaning, very close to "socialism," and they were some of the most popular programs in American history. And "right-leaning" presidents, like Eisenhower, were comfortable very near the center of that spectrum, and well within the Overton Window.

However, since the 1970's, our politicians have been edging that Overton Window to the right, little by little. By 2016, the Overton Window had shifted so far to the right, that even moderately liberal policies began to look "extreme." It is why George W. Bush was able to push ideas that were bordering on fascism - such as the Patriot Act, domestic spying, and unauthorized wars of aggression - without much political pressure. And why Barrack Obama, who ran as a "progressive" voice of hope and change, still managed to pursue policies that would have been right-wing just 30 years ago - such as additional regime-change wars, unprecedented extrajudicial killings with Predator Drones, and bank and Wall Street bailouts with tax-payer money. The Overton Window of 2016 made traditional liberal values seem more like communist propaganda.

But Bernie Sanders came along in 2015, with his first bid for the presidency. Sanders had no delusions that he would actually win. Very few people outside of his home state of Vermont knew who the bombastic Senator was. The few times he appeared on national newsfeeds, he was referred to comically as the "socialist" Senator from Vermont. But he surprised himself, and a lot of other people too - mostly establishment Democrats - when he began pulling huge crowds of cheering supporters. And even more so when he caused the closest Iowa primary race in history, and when actually won the New Hampshire primary. Sanders' rise in popularity in such a short time was truly exceptional. He went from an 80 point deficit in the fall of 2015 to being nearly tied with Clinton in national polls by spring. Sanders was able to build a truly miraculous movement against all odds, with the Democratic party openly hostile to him, and the major media outlets practically ignoring his entire campaign. And perhaps most impressively, Sanders managed to fund his campaign almost entirely with small, private donations from individual citizens, refusing to take any money from large corporate donors or Super PACs. He received a record-breaking 6 million individual contributions, averaging just $27.00 each.

Sanders has energized a huge portion of the American electorate that was previously absent from the political process. Young people and independents turn out in droves to listen to Sanders, and he enjoys a huge advantage in these demographics. His rallies draw crowds of thousands, selling out large arenas around the country. And he is responsible for enlivening debate on the frank inequality that pervades in our political and economic systems.

The fact that support is so strong for Sanders signifies a discontent with the status quo. Sanders is not exactly a "marquee" candidate, if you know what I mean. He IS a nice guy and has generally high favorability ratings, especially when considering traits such as honesty and trustworthiness. But it is his message that reverberates so loudly with a substantial segment of the populace. Working people, struggling college students, or recent graduates who are being suffocated by student loan debt, millennials who are struggling in a market with flat wages and lack of job growth, and progressive liberals who are disconcerted with the system, all rally behind Sanders because his message means something to them. And the more people that actually hear his message, the more people agree that it is time to change the way we conduct ourselves in this democracy.

Bernie's message is really quite simple - let's get money out of politics, so that the rich and powerful aren't the only ones with a voice in our government; let's provide a basic level of support to ALL Americans, including healthcare and education, which should both be considered universal human rights; let's require the wealthiest Americans and huge corporations to pay their fair share of taxes; and let's re-invigorate the middle class, and make our economy work for everyone, not just the top 1%. These are not revolutionary ideas - in fact they were classic American ideals during America's most prosperous era between 1940 and 1970. These ideals were cast aside in the 1980's, and the effects have been a disappearing middle class, unprecedented wealth inequality, and a government that no longer works for the majority of Americans. While these ideas are not revolutionary, it is going to take a revolution to re-instill them into our society, since the wealthy elites are so invested in the current failing system that they will do whatever it takes to resist going back to a time when all Americans were beneficiaries of that great "American Dream."

The establishment Democrats represent a gradualist approach to change. They still exist and function within the narrow field of the right-leaning Overton Window. While they may give lip service to the progressive liberal values of our nation's greatest modern leaders, they too are infected by the interests that promote the current system. They too are betrothed to the wealthy elites, funding their campaigns with Wall Street donations, and thus being careful not to bite the hand that feeds them. They too are compelled to military action around the globe in order to protect the interests of a handful of rich and powerful donors, at the expense of working class people. They too are embroiled in the military-industrial complex, the mass incarceration culture, and the almost criminally overpriced pharmaceutical and healthcare syndicate, all of which profits the rich but impoverishes everyone else. The tiny, incremental steps that these establishment politicians promise do nothing but perpetuate the inequality and unfairness of the current system.

But something dramatic is happening in this country. While just two years ago these establishment politicians would have us believe that equality, fairness, economic opportunity, and fundamental human rights are just a fantasy, the current list of presidential hopefuls are singing a new song. While Clinton and her Democratic party called single-payer, universal healthcare a pipe dream; and tuition-free public universities "pie in the sky"; and providing economic opportunity and a living wage to all hard-working Americans idealistic and unrealistic - these exact same policies are now on the lips, and indeed the platforms, of most of the Democratic contenders for 2020. Amazingly, in just two short years, the party that laughed at Medicare for All, calling it a "pony," is now supporting several candidates that claim to support just such a radical program.

Bernie Sanders did this. Bernie Sanders has shown us that all these things can be accomplished. He has shown us that by raising the standard of living of America's poor and working class that our country can be better for ALL Americans. He has brought to light the simple fact that fairness and equality will benefit both beneficiary and benefactor alike. And he has reminded us that these ideas are not some new, unrealistic fantasy, but that they used to be core American values that made the country - at one time - the envy of the entire world. He continues to highlight the fact that the policies of the past 30 years have completely failed MOST Americans, causing the poor to get poorer, the middle class to practically disappear, and the rich to become a smaller and smaller club of elites.

No other candidate was talking about these things in 2016. But in the 2018 mid-term elections, we saw rising stars such as Alexandria Ocasio-Cortez, Rashida Tlaib and Ilhan Omar win historic Congressional victories. The Progressive Caucus in Congress has grown bigger and more powerful, and Bernie Sanders' own organization, Our Revolution - led by voracious Bernie supporter and Ohio State Senator Nina Turner - has been running candidates in elections big and small across the country. The Progressive movement has taken hold, reinvigorated electoral politics, and brought youth and enthusiasm to the polls, thereby shoving the Overton Window leftward by a significant margin.

However, without Bernie Sanders, and the revolution that he brought with him, progressive issues would likely be buried back down in the sands of history, and the status quo would once again be touted as the American Dream. Bernie Sanders has remained active and outspoken and continues to spread his message, and continues to inspire millions to demand a new New Deal. His efforts are forcing the Democratic Party to re-adopt the progressive views of its past, and to realign with the values of liberals. So whether or not Bernie Sanders throws his hat back in the ring in 2020 - something myself and countless other progressives sincerely hope he will do - he has already won a decisive victory in America. Bernie Sanders, with the help and support of grassroots activists and progressive leaders across the country, has managed to undo decades of rightward shift of America's Overton Window. If Bernie Sanders runs in 2020, he will win. But even if he doesn't, we have real, progressive alternatives that are running exactly because Bernie Sanders showed the way. So either way, Bernie will win in 2020, because his ideas, and his movement, have made today's progressive values possible. #RunBernieRun #Bernie2020

CHAPTER THREE
Political Parties

"There is nothing I dread so much as the division of the republic into two great parties, each arranged under its leader, and concerting measures in opposition to each other. This, in my humble apprehension, is to be dreaded as the greatest political evil under our constitution."

\- John Adams

VIII.
Political Party Revolution

In the summer of 1776, at what was perhaps the height of the American Revolution, the Thirteen Colonies of America declared their independence from British rule. It is interesting to note that the United States was officially born when the Second Continental Congress voted for a resolution of independence on July 2, 1776. In fact, John Adams, who would later become the new nation's second president, wrote a letter stating that July 2 would "be the most memorable epoch in the history of America," and that it would "be celebrated by succeeding generations as the great anniversary festival." However, the "Committee of Five" drafted the Declaration of Independence, which was simply a written statement explaining the decision made on July 2, and it was approved and (allegedly) signed on July 4, and it is this day that the country has always celebrated as it's Independence Day.

Fun Fact: Three presidents in a row - John Adams, Thomas Jefferson, and James Monroe - all died on July 4. Adams and Jefferson, both of whom signed the Declaration of Independence, actually died on the same day, July 4, 1826, the nation's 50th Anniversary. Monroe died 5 years later in 1831.

20 years after our nation's first Independence Day, on September 19, 1796, George Washington, the nation's first President, gave his farewell speech after serving two terms in the White House. Well, not the White House, as it wasn't built yet, but the 'President's

House' in Philadelphia, which he occupied from 1790 until 1797. In his final address to the fledgling nation, Washington advocated a non-partisan government. He was worried that "factions" and political parties were dangerous and would weaken the government. He reasoned that parties have a tendency to "gradually incline the minds of men to seek security and repose in the absolute power of an individual." Thus, the "alternate domination" of one party over another "is itself a frightful despotism. But . . . leads at length to a more formal and permanent despotism." In other words, political parties tend to start out corrupted and get more corrupted over time, wrenching control of the government from the people and placing it in the hands of the parties - or more accurately, the hands of the undemocratic, unelected party elites.

Despite the wisdom of President Washington's impassioned plea, partisanship ensued practically the moment he left office. Despite having written letters denouncing political parties, Alexander Hamilton became one of the founders of the Federalist Party, which advocated a strong central government and centralized banking. Shortly thereafter, Thomas Jefferson helped to create the Democratic-Republican Party, also known as the "Anti-Federalist" party. The Democratic-Republicans espoused state's rights, and a small federal government, and grew out of opposition to the "Federalists," which included Hamilton, James Madison, and John Adams. Between 1792 and 1824, what has become known as the First Party System produced fierce partisanship, including the presidential election of 1800, which has been referred to as "one of the most acrimonious in the annals of American history."

Ever since political parties first invaded American politics, with minuscule exception, the party system has persisted. And for most of that time, we have been laboring under the same 2-party system that we have today. Democrats and Republicans, the dominant parties in American politics, have controlled Congress and the White House since the 1850's. Over that time, there have been several fundamental shifts and realignments within the parties. The Fifth Party System, which began around 1933 with Franklin Roosevelt's "New Deal," is arguably the era we still fit within. Beginning around that time, the Democratic Party, led by Roosevelt, became the party of American Liberalism, promoting progressive values and social welfare. Meanwhile, the Republican Party was split fairly evenly between conservatives and moderates.

However, many argue that our current era should be considered the Sixth Party System, beginning around 1964 with Lyndon Johnson's presidency and the Civil Rights movement. It was around this time that Democrats, once known as the pro-slavery party, became the party of equal rights for African Americans. This caused a fundamental ideological shift in both parties, when white Southern men, who had been a core component of the Democratic Party, abandoned the party *en masse* in favor of the Republican Party.

Since this re-alignment of values, the parties have continued to evolve. Republicans have continued to grow more and more conservative, while the Democrats, at least since Bill Clinton's presidency, have followed along. What is also becoming increasingly clear is that the parties themselves - or, more accurately, the undemocratic, unelected party elites themselves - have become both powerful and corrupt in the intervening years. And these same parties that have dominated for more than a century and a half, are increasingly less representative of the people they claim to represent.

The 2016 election cycle, if anything, acted as sort of herald of the growing discontent of the American people with the dominant 2-party system. More voters in the U.S. identify as "Independent" - or 'no party preference' - than identify as either of the two major parties - significantly so. Approximately 45% of Americans now refer to themselves as independents - a new high - while Republican affiliation is at a paltry 27% and Democrats are barely leading with 28%. Moreover, almost 60% of Americans polled agree that we need a viable third party. There is clearly resentment growing amongst a large percentage of this nation's populace with the entrenched party establishment.

Jeffrey Jones of Gallup had this to say:

"The rise in political independence is likely related to Americans' frustration with party gridlock in the federal government. In the past several years, dissatisfaction with the government has ranked among the leading issues when U.S. adults are asked to name the most important problem facing the U.S., and was the most frequently mentioned problem in 2014 and 2015."

There no doubt have been, and will yet be entire books, dissertations and essays explaining the reasons Americans feel left out of - or left behind by - the political system as it exists today. It is, in fact, difficult to even offer a "short" answer to this question. There are many issues which frustrate the average American voter, including the proliferation of money in politics, corruption, scandals, stagnant do-nothing lawmakers, and politicians who blatantly ignore public opinion in favor of corporate and/or ideological interests, to name just a few. And the number of Americans that believe the two dominant parties adequately represent Americans' interests is at an all-time low - less than 25%.

Well, the good news is that we don't have to take it. There is no Constitutional provision for the existence of political parties, and there is no requirement that our elected officials belong to any particular party. There are currently numerous congressmen, governors, and state politicians across the country that identify as Independent, or are members of a third party. Lincoln Chafee was elected governor of Rhode Island in 2010 as an Independent; Bernie Sanders, elected in 1990 for his first term in the House of Representatives, is the longest serving Independent in Congress; Joe Lieberman switched his party status to a third -party in 2006 while running for the Senate; Angus King, Senator from Maine, is an independent; and there are numerous members of state legislatures that are either independent or third-party. In other words, there is no legal impediment to abandoning the current two-party system.

Admittedly, there are fierce political obstacles, but they are, hopefully, not insurmountable. Ballot access laws, debate rules, and most importantly our winner-take-all "plurality" voting system are the largest hindrances to third party candidates. But these systems can be changed if enough people are committed to making it happen. We need lawmakers to amend ballot requirements and debate rules, and we need voter education and referenda to address the way we conduct elections at both the state and national level. And we of course need voters who aren't afraid to abandon a political party that has long since abandoned them. We need voters to back third party candidates in elections big and small.

And now is the time to do it, while we have historic levels of voter dissatisfaction, and government leaders that don't even pretend to care what voters think. And while we have a huge portion of the American electorate clamoring for something outside the two-party, Washington establishment. Considering the level of disenchantment (and virtual disenfranchisement) we may just have the momentum to move forward. When a significant percentage of Americans actually voted for Donald Trump - a maniac, to be sure, but someone his supporters saw as the "anti-status quo" candidate - it is a clear indication that the status quo needs to be changed. If the best choices our broken two-party system can give us is a sneaky, corrupted establishment hack (which could be said about any of the popular Democratic establishment hopefuls for 2020), and a blustering, bumbling, anti-intellectual bigot, I would strongly suggest that now is the time for action. American politics cannot continue being a team sport, especially when both teams are owned by the same special interests.

IX.
Gary Johnson & Glass Houses

The 2016 presidental election became, at some point, a tragic comedy. A foul-mouthed, bumbling buffoon. A hypocritical, underhanded war monger. A psychopathic, misogynistic white supremacist. And a Wall Street wolf wearing ill-fitting sheep's clothing. Or, Trump, Clinton, Pence and Kaine respectively. This clown car of deplorables engaged in a shock and awe campaign of open warfare against each other, and unfortunately the health, wealth and posterity of our entire nation may be unavoidable collateral damage. How did we get here?

The simple answer is that the parties really dropped the ball on this one. The Republicans are such a piebald and petty collection of narcissistic prima donnas that they couldn't rally enough support around a single candidate to beat Trump in the primaries. Remember that Republican primary field? There were enough conservative white men on that stage to start a new NRA chapter - and Dr. Ben Carson was there, too. But because of the fractured nature of the Republican party, they couldn't beat the ridiculous spectacle that is Donald Trump. Pox on you, Republicans.

And the Democrats weren't much better. Before the primary season even began, the Democratic National Committee already decided that Hillary Clinton would be the party's nominee. Hillary Clinton - who even then was known as one of the most unlikeable public figures in modern history - was selected by party elites to lead the party. They were so blinded by loyalty to Hillary that they completely ignored the majority of probable voters - both Democrats and Independents - that made it very clear that Clinton was not acceptable. With a much smaller field, and a handful of rather promising candidates, the DNC still chose (by essentially rigging the primaries) the absolute worst candidate of the bunch - well, not counting Jim Webb. So, pox on you too, Democrats.

Because of severe dysfunction within the parties themselves, we ended up with the two most unfavorable major party candidates in history heading into the November election. And its not just the Donald's uncanny resemblance to an orange orangutan, or Hillary's irritating penchant for designer pantsuits. Both of these people are deeply flawed, and have decades of verifiable history which demonstrate - loudly - those flaws.

Of course the big news this week was the revelation of Trump's "hot mic" moment with Billy Bush when he suggested that celebrities could sexually assault women without reprisal. The candid moment was obviously horrifying to any modern sensibility and an assault to common decency. The Trump camp has tried to assuage the impact of the interview by stating that it was "locker room talk" and that it occurred more than a decade ago - in 2005. First, are they trying to say that Trump is not the same person he was when he was only 60 years old? Has he honestly changed and "matured" that much between his 60th and 70th birthdays? Not likely. And while I will grant some degree of credence to the "locker room" nature of the comments - since, as a man I have heard some pretty tasteless and objectifying talk about women in locker rooms - I have to draw the line at literally condoning sexual battery. But here is the question I have for all the former Trump supporters that have since jumped ship, as well as all the liberals who are foaming at the mouth at such a vulgar display of predatory misogyny - Is anyone actually surprised? I mean, we have all known what a pig Trump is for years.

What I find most compelling about this backroom banter is the timing of its release - at almost the exact instant that Wikileaks released emails from the Clinton campaign. And of course, the salacity of Trump's toilet talk has practically buried the rather damning emails concerning Hillary and her henchmen. If anyone was paying attention, we got to see some of the statements Hillary made to Wall Street executives in speeches for which she was paid millions of dollars, including some very telling insights into her actual political positions. For instance she admitted that she has no idea what it's like for the middle class - in other words, she is completely out of touch with common folk and is much more interested in helping the wealthy. She also stated that she has "public positions" and "private positions," essentially promising Wall Street favors while publicly pretending to be tough on them. In addition to the numerous nuggets of hypocrisy and underhandedness revealed by the email dump, it also became clearer that Clinton and the mainstream media are and have been actively conspiring to undermine this election. I could ask the same question - Is anyone surprised - but the more pressing question is why wasn't everyone more concerned about these revelations? Well, because Trump. They always find a way to put the spotlight back on him.

This whole election cycle has been one big mud fight, with all the candidates focused more on showing how terrible the other candidates are than actually discussing the issues. And as the field has narrowed, we have emerged with two major party candidates that both seem to be running with the slogan "I'm Better Than The Other Guy." The problem is that both of these candidates are throwing stones from their own glass houses. Admittedly, Trump does seem to have worse aim, actually throwing a few stones at his own house along the way, but Hillary remains just as vulnerable to people who are actually paying attention. And if we continue going down this road, we really will have a president that is elected because slightly more than half the population hates one candidate slightly less than the other one. This is not how democracy is supposed to work.

And then there's Gary Johnson. I only bring this guy up for all you "conscientious" conservatives out there that can no longer vote for Trump because he has a potty mouth. It is no secret that I cannot - will not - vote for Hillary Clinton, even though I think a Trump presidency could possibly lead to the end of modern civilization. In other words, I believe it would be good for America - and the rest of the world - if *neither* of our major party candidates wins in November. And while I will likely cast a protest vote for Jill Stein myself, I acknowledge that the Green Party is not quite ready to cause any significant upset to our current 2-party system. Which is why I mention Gary Johnson, the Libertarian candidate. I'm no supporter of Johnson and his *laissez-faire* economic policy proposals, but I would much prefer a Johnson-Weld win over a Trump-Pence win.

Gary Johnson is not the brightest bulb in the chandelier, to be sure. But he espouses a position that most economic conservatives should be fawning over. He also stands for many of the social policy positions that more liberal-minded voters would welcome, including pro-choice abortion policy, ending the war on drugs and mass incarceration, and marriage equality. And while his foreign policy expertise is - lacking? - his non-interventionist position would save billions of dollars and thousands of American lives. And while this guy is not so smart, he is at least as smart as Trump, who comes across as barely literate. So, why don't you Republicans vote for Gary Johnson? He is already polling at well over 10%, meaning he has a real chance of causing an upset, especially if Trump supporters abandon Trump *en masse* and switch to the Libertarian ticket.

And while I would have many problems with a Johnson presidency, if we really are running a "lesser evil" campaign, then I gotta say that he would probably be less damaging - and less evil - than either Trump or Hillary, regardless of which side of the aisle you are currently seated. So, let's let the two big parties continue to tear each other's houses down to the ground, and elect a third party candidate to office for the first time in history. It will not only avert a catastrophe of biblical proportions, it will also pave the way for a ruling class that actually listens to its constituencies. A Johnson-Weld win, while less than ideal, may just save our beloved democracy from utter collapse.

X.
Spoiler Warning: The Green Party

IN 2016 I was able to vote my conscience. I chose to vote for a woman, because frankly it is high time we had one in the Oval Office, after 240 years of male dominance over the levers of power in this great nation. However, I did not vote for a woman just because she is a woman - that would be just as sexist as voting for a man just because he's <u>not</u> a woman. I voted for a woman who I believe displays integrity, honesty, compassion and a solid core of democratic values. Of course you have probably guessed by now that I did not vote for Hillary Clinton, because she has none of those things. I voted for Dr. Jill Stein, the Green Party candidate, because I could not bring myself to vote for either of the major party candidates. I had the privilege of being able to vote third party without any guilt. Living in a dark red state, my vote for a Democratic presidential candidate is just as wasted as not voting at all. So I was able to do this act of defiance without any consequences.

For the first time in 24 years, I voted for a party other than my beloved Democratic Party. I de-registered as a Democrat following the blatant dishonesty of the 2016 primaries, in spite of my decades-long loyalty thereto. I voted Green Party not because I have decided to join the Green Party - I have not, and will remain as a declared Independent for the time being. And I didn't necessarily vote Green because I actually want Jill Stein as our next president. Don't get me wrong, I think Dr. Stein would be a far greater choice than any of the other candidates on that ballot, but that is not really the point. I voted Green precisely because there **are no** good choices for president this year. I voted for a third party because we **need** a third party to encourage better choices.

We were provided with the opportunity in 2016 to vote for the two most undesirable candidates in history. The Democratic Party virtually guaranteed that the voice of the people mattered little, if any, in selecting our candidate, and instead foisted a well-known liar, opportunist and thoroughly corrupt candidate upon its members. The Republican Party didn't do much better, by bitter infighting and absolutist ideology, they allowed a thoroughly unelectable monster to become their nominee. And then, because of the way we run elections in this country, they insisted that we must make our choice between these two despicable people, or else we are "wasting our vote." Don't buy into that argument, ladies and gentlemen. Voting your conscience is never a wasted vote, and never has that been more clear and important than now.

We need - and we deserve - choices. Real choices, not the "Hobson's Choice" we have been given in recent years. The reason that we are reduced to, year after year, voting for the "lesser of two evils" is that we are not given but two, usually evil, choices. And as long as we continue to play ball and pull that less evil lever, we are surrendering our own will to the will of the rich and powerful that control our government, media and elections. But if we actually assert our collective will, we can change this. For once, abandon short-term complacence and vote for permanent change. For once, send a message to the entrenched power structure that we, not they, are in charge. For once, stop following the herd, and vote outside the circle of Washington vultures for the chance of dethroning the corrupt, back-biting, selfish and elitist criminals that run our two major political parties.

I did not vote Green because I think the Green Party will overtake the Democrats any time soon. I did it because if enough people do, we may be able to introduce the viability of third parties in national elections. I did it because if enough people indicate that they are finished with this two-party system that is so clearly and thoroughly bought and paid for by the wealthy masters of finance and industry, we may just have a chance at uprooting that corrupt, pay-for-play system. They are the grasshoppers, and we are the ants - if enough of us realize that we overwhelmingly outnumber them, we can take our country back.

I am tired of voting for the slightly-less-detestable candidate. Hillary Clinton may not be the murderer or criminal that the right-wing suggests. But don't patronize me by saying that I bought into conspiracy theories about Clinton when I call her corrupt. Don't pretend not to notice that, while she may not have been convicted of high crimes and misdemeanors, she has a well-verified history of hypocrisy, corruption, and a complete lack of ethics. And she also has a verifiable record of failures that greatly outnumber any alleged successes. Smart people know that Hillary Clinton is a corporatist, and an elitist, and thinks only about herself and her wealthy elite "friends" every time she opens her mouth. And don't give me that shit, "Well, that's how politics goes," or some such other tired argument. If that's how politics goes, then that is a problem, because its not supposed to be how politics goes. Don't forget that "politics" is what governs our nation, and the only losers in that system are us, the voters, the bottom 90% of the country. We lose every time we are forced to vote against our conscience to avoid a disaster like Donald Trump. We lose every time our government ignores the will of the majority of Americans to appease some wealthy and powerful special interest. And if we continue to allow this type of hijacking to go un-policed, we risk losing our rights altogether. I voted third party because I could, and I should, and because it is my duty as an American to challenge the status quo, especially when the status quo is so clearly antithetical to the preservation of American democracy.

CHAPTER FOUR
Law Enforcement Reform

"Unless the powerful are capable of learning to respect the dignity of their victims, impassable barriers will remain, and the world will be doomed to violence, cruelty, and bitter suffering."

- Noam Chomsky

XI.
Predation versus Prevention

It is no secret that America is the Incarceration Capital of the world. Not only does the U.S. have the highest percentage of prison inmates, we also have the highest absolute number of citizens behind bars. In fact, while the U.S. population makes up only 5% of the world's population, we boast nearly 25% of the world's prisoners. There are more than two million people in state and federal prisons, and another half-million in local jails. Additionally, there are another 5 million or so people on probation or parole, bringing the total number of Americans under correctional supervision to more than 7 million Americans. That is approximately 3% of all adults in the country. And to be sure, those staggering numbers have allowed the growth of a massive law enforcement and corrections industry, which generates billions of dollars each year - as long as the business keeps coming in.

But it hasn't always been this way. There was a time in America, probably before my lifetime, when the law enforcement community included minimally-armed patrolling officers, "walking the beat." The ideal - at least from childhood television - was of friendly and helpful policemen strolling the streets of the neighborhood, ready to respond if something seemed fishy, and ready to help if someone needed assistance. The conventional wisdom was that if there is a benign police presence, crimes of opportunity would be less likely to occur. As the old adage suggests, an ounce of prevention is worth a pound of cure.

Somewhere along the line, first in the 1960's with the Civil Rights movement, and more so in the 1970's with the newly-declared War on Drugs, crime prevention became much less important than catching criminals and locking them up. As police departments became more and more militarized, and socio-economic divisions grew, creating uglier pockets of poverty and desperation, even-tempered community policing turned swiftly into overtly aggressive, paramilitary law enforcement. And alongside this shift in police focus we saw the rise of the Prison Industrial Complex, which encourages, at least covertly, a constant flow of human capital in the form of prisoners. And damn the cost to the lives of those caught up in its ever-expanding net.

Instead of crime deterrence, we began to see the advent of security measures designed to trap criminals in the act. Silent Alarms, hidden cameras, speed traps and road blocks (euphemistically referred to as 'Sobriety Checkpoints"). For example, it is not uncommon for police officers to surveil a local nightclub, and watch drunk patrons leave. Instead of intervening when they see an obviously inebriated person heading for their car, they wait until the person gets in the car, and drives away, thereby needlessly endangering the community, just so they can make the arrest. For the past 40+ years, law enforcement, security companies, and even private businesses have been devising new ways to apprehend criminals, catching them in the act if at all possible, instead of trying to deter a would-be criminal beforehand. Plainclothes officers cruise around in unmarked cars for the sole purpose of not announcing a police presence - not that it's hard to tell an unmarked car in most instances, but it is still less conspicuous than a marked cruiser. And it sends the same signal - we aren't here to prevent crime, we're here to observe it.

In my experience, one of the most ubiquitous techniques used by police officers is the confidential informant and, specifically with narcotics officers, the controlled buy. C.I.s are recruited by the police to report any criminal activity they observe. They often have their own criminal history, and often become a C.I. to garner favorable treatment or for some other quid pro quo, like money. The C.I. is almost always known to the community, and is therefore able to interact with suspects in ways that police officers, or strangers, could not. They may even be able to go inside someone's home and inform the police if there is any contraband in the home, like guns or drugs. Basically, it is a way for police to violate the Fourth Amendment prohibition against warrantless searches, without actually conducting a warrantless search. They will then use the information provided by the C.I. to obtain a search warrant. And while this makes the confidential informant a key witness in a case, it can be very difficult to force the state to disclose their identity, and often a criminal defendant is prevented from confronting and cross-examining the C.I. at trial.

Police will also use a C.I. to conduct a "controlled buy" of narcotics from someone the police believe is selling drugs. Again, the C.I. is usually someone the alleged drug dealer knows personally. Police will give the C.I. marked money, have him make the buy, and bring the purchased narcotics back to the police. And again, based on this secret transaction, the police will obtain a search warrant and/or an arrest warrant for the drug dealer. Oftentimes, while conducting surveillance of the target residence, officers will watch several people buy narcotics and leave, which they will use as additional evidence against the perpetrator. But that means that they are literally allowing people to continue buying narcotics, putting more drugs on the street, just to build a stronger case against the dealer.

One particular case stands out in my mind. My client was a known drug addict, and had been arrested and convicted of several drug charges in the past, mostly for simple possession - because he was a drug addict. Cops employed a confidential informant that knew my client to try and conduct a controlled buy from him. In a recorded conversation, the C.I. called my client and asked for some crack. My client said he didn't have any. The C.I. asked him again, and again my client said he wasn't selling any. For several minutes, this continued on, with the C.I. practically begging my client for just one piece of crack for an old friend. My client finally relented, and agreed to give him one - as an old friend. He was arrested and charged with Distribution of Schedule II narcotics, punishable by up to 30 years in prison. However, because of his criminal history, if my client had gone to trial and been found guilty, he was likely facing Life Without Parole. So he was forced into a plea bargain which required him to serve at least 7 years in prison.

Another of the more despicable techniques used by law enforcement to catch criminals is the relatively new practice of "Bait Cars." Police will park a nice car in a "high crime" area, leaving the keys in the ignition. Inside the car, there are hidden cameras. When some kid comes by and sees the keys in it, they take it for a spin. And of course, they are then arrested and charged with Theft of an Automobile - or Grand Theft Auto, depending on where you are. I even had a case where the police staged a DWI arrest in a poor neighborhood, arrested the fake driver, and left the scene, with the car - a very nice, new "cool" car - in the middle of the street with the keys still in the ignition. My client was a 17-year old kid who was walking with his friends when he observed this staged arrest. He and one of his buddies hopped in the car and drove it around for a few minutes. They had no intention of keeping the car, but just planned to drive it around and return it when they were done. This used to be called "joyriding" and was punishable as a misdemeanor. But now, at least in Louisiana, it is treated exactly the same as any other car theft, a felony, punishable by up to ten years in prison.

These tactics, among others, are often colloquially referred to as "proactive" policing. I have seen countless police reports that begin with the copied and pasted phrase "while on proactive patrol, officers observed [fill in the blank]." Sometimes it just means creeping through "bad" neighborhoods, looking for a fight or a group of 'suspicious' looking people - most often young, black men. Sometimes, they take advantage of a known drug addict, asking them to buy some crack for them, in exchange for money, or some of the crack. The addict may comply, desperate for his own fix, and seek out someone to buy from. When he returns with the product, he is arrested for distribution. Sometimes, plainclothes cops attempt to entrap prostitutes into offering sex for money, just so they can make the arrest. And there are numerous other methods modern police officers use to persuade at-risk people into committing crimes, just so they can arrest them, and lock them up. And, somehow, all of these tactics have survived scrutiny under entrapment defenses. In fact, it has become increasingly difficult to prove entrapment in American courts, and it is always the defendant's burden of proof when making such a claim.

Instead of focusing on community policing, which would place a constant benign police presence in neighborhoods, it is easier - and more profitable - to "proactively" induce criminal behavior, or to lay in wait until someone commits a crime, and then pounce, attacking the perpetrator like an enemy combatant. My wife says it reminds her of 'ambush predators' on the African savanna, and I thought that was the most apt description available. Modern American cops are more akin to ambush predators than friendly neighborhood police officers. And of course, the communities that suffer the most negative impact of this type of regressive policing are vulnerable groups, such as racial minorities and the working poor. Communities that have been systematically segregated to the "bad" parts of town, where most "proactive policing" is centered, already struggle to get by, and are hamstrung by regressive law enforcement policies that target them.

Of course there is a much longer conversation to be had about the underlying causes of crime, which include socio-economic depression and desperation. Drug addicts are often created by poverty and hopelessness, as well as undiagnosed and/or untreated mental illness. Illicit drug sales are often concentrated in areas where these factors are most patent, such as poor, working class communities, which are often communities of color. Thefts, robberies, burglaries, assaults and firefights are often concentrated around those same neighborhoods, for most of the same reasons. Poor people, with no hope of breaking out of poverty, resort to desperate measures just to get by. We only make matters worse with idealistic expectations of beauty and success in popular culture and mass media. But these issues will take more long-term, bolder and more nuanced policies to fully address. However, we can ease some of the burden on these already-at-risk communities by demanding a more preventative approach to law enforcement, instead of trapping marginalized people into committing crimes of opportunity, just to feed more customers into the nation's overstuffed prison system, thereby perpetuating the cycle of poverty to desperation to crime and back to prison. But then again, that wouldn't fit the modern business model of the Prison Industrial Complex, and all of its enablers.

XII.
Bipartisan Fascism

Being a police officer is a tough job. No doubt about it. Our boys in blue put their lives on the line to protect us from society's most destructive elements. In the past decade, about 140 police officers were killed in the line of duty each year. Most of those men and women died with honor, serving their communities, and deserve our sympathy and support. All of that is true. Police officers do put their lives on the line - because that is exactly what they are hired to do. That is exactly what they sign up for. It is a commitment, and often times a sacrifice, and we appreciate it - but that's what they are supposed to do. And we support them - we pay their salary, purchase equipment, give them benefits, special protections from civil liability, and much more. In exchange for society's support of law enforcement, we expect them to be professional, brave and compassionate guardians of our citizens. We expect them to be honest, and exercise good judgment, and above all - as the motto suggests - to protect and serve the public.

Somewhere along the line, we have gotten off track with our expectations of police officers. Especially if you are a marginalized group, such as minorities, you have become especially wary of law enforcement in recent years. Communities of color often come to dread the presence of police, due to numerous and repeated incidents concerning unwarranted, unprofessional and often excessive violence by police against unarmed civilians. Since the

1970's, the traditional role of law enforcement has been supplanted by a domestic para-military strike force as a response to the newly-declared War on Drugs (which has been an utter failure and the subject of a later discussion). The drug war, and all the benefits it has brought with it, has led to aggressive policing. The perpetual combat engaged in by law enforcement has led to the militarization of police departments around the country, which, as can be easily imagined, has only made matters worse.

The Department of Justice's Edward Byrne Memorial Justice Assistance Grant Program, and the Department of Defense's 1033 program, among others, have armed local law enforcement agencies with military and para-military equipment. Armored Personnel Carriers, flashbang grenades, and assault rifles, combined with aggressive training and tactics, have made police officers into combatants in a war, instead of public servants on our city streets. In fact, in many instances police officers are encouraged through their training to adopt a "warrior" mentality, and to "think of the people they are supposed to serve as enemies."

Special Weapons and Tactics (SWAT) teams were originally adopted to handle emergency situations, such as hostage crises. However, today nearly 2/3 of SWAT deployments involve simple drug raids. They serve search warrants on the suspicion that someone may be in possession of drugs, often a small amount. These para-military SWAT teams break down doors in the middle of the night, with battering rams, toss grenades into the house to blind and deafen the occupants, and enter, full assault style, to serve a search warrant. As should be expected, there is a greatly increased risk of violence in these raids, which are violent events in themselves.

Many police officers are honest, hard-working men and women. They perform heroic acts, and place themselves willingly in danger. But even these good officers are trained, armed and ordered to conduct aggressive, "proactive" policing, especially in "high crime" areas that are often neighborhoods of color. Police officers are sent into these areas to look for a fight, and to engage the public as enemy combatants. Is it any wonder that there are so many police shootings, when they are whipped into a frenzy and conditioned to be on high-alert at every moment?

The response has been, for the past few decades, a quiet acquiescence to the increase in police use of force. We were conditioned by the establishment to accept this new policing as being "tough on crime." We were taught to think of every two-bit street hustler and pot smoker as a dangerous criminal that must be handled with extreme prejudice. But in recent years, more and more conscientious observers have begun to remonstrate. We saw organized protests in Ferguson, Missouri after police shot and killed an unarmed Michael Brown; demonstrations in Baton Rouge, Louisiana after the shooting death of another unarmed black man, Alton sterling; and the emergence of Black Lives Matter, an activist movement that campaigns against violence and systemic racism. And these protesters have every right to voice their grievances, which are valid and legitimate grievances. The same police that citizens pay to protect them have too often violated their rights, threatened, harassed and even killed them outright, frequently for minor - or even non-existent - infractions (such as the case of Philando

Castille).

In response to this outcry against aggressive policing, law enforcement advocates have declared that there is now some imaginary "War on Cops." 'Law and Order' politicians from both sides of the political spectrum have derided community efforts to improve police/citizen relations by insisting that the police have a job to do. They support and defend officers that physically attack, shoot or kill criminal suspects, suggesting that if arrestees would simply cooperate, there would be no need for violence. In other words, time after time, the victim is blamed for his own situation. Because we are all expected by law enforcement, and their enablers, to submit unquestioningly to authority. And this is simply not what a democracy is supposed to look like.

In fact, it is a rather jealously guarded right - in most states - for citizens to resist an unlawful arrest, with reasonable force if necessary. Any limit on the citizens to resist unlawful conduct by police officers, is a direct, flagrant, and frightening violation of the Fourth Amendment right to be free from "unreasonable searches and seizures." And yes, an arrest, or even a brief detention, is a "seizure," and "unlawful" is the same as "unreasonable." In most states, and at common law, the right to resist an unlawful arrest is sacrosanct, for precisely that reason – it is consistent with our Fourth Amendment rights. For example, in *City of Monroe v. Ducas*, a Louisiana court reversed the relators' convictions under a local ordinance making it unlawful to resist a police officer in the discharge of his duties. Michael and John Ducas, members of a religious organization, had called at the home of a black family for the purpose of taking them to a bible study class. This activity impressed a police officer as "dangerous and suspicious" conduct, and he approached relators, demanding to know what they were doing. When Michael Ducas replied that "it was none of [the officer's] business" and attempted to drive away, the officer tried to stop him and was injured. Observing that the relators had not been guilty of violating any law at the time of their arrest, the Court declared: "*The right of personal liberty is one of the fundamental rights guaranteed to every citizen, and any unlawful interference with it may be resisted. Every person has a right to resist an unlawful arrest; and, in preventing such illegal restraint of his liberty, he may use such force as may be necessary.*"

However, due to the rise of anti-police violence advocacy, our federal lawmakers are attempting to limit this right, and impose a form of martial law that demands people respect and obey an officer, whether or not he is right. In a bipartisan effort - only 35 members of the House of Representatives voted against it - Congress is considering a bill, coined the "Protect and Serve Act," which would essentially make assaulting a police officer - under any condition - a federal hate crime. The bill is a response to "anti-cop" messaging which is blamed on groups like Black Lives Matter, or the national controversy surrounding kneeling NFL players. These protests of police violence are conflated with some ideological hatred for all cops, which simply isn't the case. The protesters aren't calling for an end to police officers - just unwarranted violence, and the perpetual vindication and exculpation of bad cops by the law enforcement community. The so-called 'thin blue line' serves to condone and endorse excessive force and aggressive policing, and this abomination of a law is codifying it.

The purpose of hate crime laws is to protect a vulnerable class of citizens from being targeted simply because of their inclusion in that class. As noted by Radley Blako in the Washington Post, "[t]he problem with adding police officers . . . is that they are about as far removed from a vulnerable group as one can imagine. They carry guns and other weapons. They have the power to detain, arrest and kill. And they literally have the entire government at their back." In other words, they are not a powerless and marginalized group in any way, and including them in the definition of a vulnerable class is completely idiotic.

I am assuming that the congresspeople who devised this law have no reason to believe that this type of law could ever be misused or exploited against citizens. The Senate version of the bill makes it a federal hate crime "to knowingly cause bodily injury to any person, or attempt to do so, because of the actual or perceived status of the person as a law enforcement officer." This is very broad language that makes any physical contact - or even the attempted contact - with a police officer a felony, regardless of the reason. Currently, a simple battery of a police officer is, at least in Louisiana, a misdemeanor, punishable by up to 6 months in jail. But under this bill, a simple battery of a police office could be a federal hate crime carrying up to 10 years in federal prison. This should frighten anyone who cares about civil liberties - which should be everyone. And as previously noted, the broad language of the Senate bill can certainly be read to prohibit even reasonable and necessary force against a rogue officer who is engaged in unlawful behavior.

Despite the serious potential for abuse this bill

introduces, there is simply no need for it. Most states already have special penalties for crimes against law enforcement, and such crimes are aggressively enforced. As Ilya Somin stated in Reason, "if anything, we have more reason to fear that police and prosecutors will fail to properly address crimes committed *by* police than crimes committed against them." It is also a well-documented fact that the "war on police" comes at a time when violence against police officers is at historical lows, and has been trending downward for years. Despite the pro-police rhetoric, increased public criticism of violent officers does not equate to increased violence against cops. It is a myth, and it is deliberately misleading to make this connection. And while law enforcement can be considered a dangerous profession, it is interesting to note that it doesn't even make the top 10 most dangerous jobs in America. Lawncare supervisors are more likely to die in the line of duty than police officers. There is simply no objective reason to grant another huge protection for cops at the potential expense of civil liberties.

This bill is yet another attempt to make law enforcement an unassailable force of authority in a nation that prides itself on freedom. Every valid criticism of the increased surveillance apparatus, draconian sentencing schemes and oppressive police practices is met with threats and harassment, and even chilling legislation. Protesters are branded as anti-police or unpatriotic. But this is simply wrong. Unpatriotic would be to allow, with no opposition, a takeover by the police state, surrender of our civil liberties, and an end to democratic and constitutional values such as free speech, free press, and the freedom of assembly. Protesters are exercising their rights, and defending their rights to criticize and admonish the power structures that are, supposedly, designed to serve us, not oppress us. I sincerely hope sensible minds prevail on this atrocious bill which seemingly criminalizes lawful resistance. But so far, it appears that there is a bi-partisan coalition of pandering, bootlicking politicians using this fascistic law to grandstand and highlight their "pro-police" positions. This type of law is a waypoint on a road toward toward fascism, and with so many congressmen, from both sides of aisle, supporting such measures, we may get to the end of the road sooner than any of us think.

CHAPTER FIVE
The War on Drugs

"If you support the war on drugs in its present form, then you're only paying lip-service to the defense of freedom, and you don't really grasp the concept of the sovereign individual human being."

- Neil Boortz

XIII.
Black versus Blue:
Brought to you by the War on Drugs

Beginning a few years ago, in August 2014, an unarmed Michael Brown was gunned down by a police officer in Ferguson, Missouri. While this was nothing new, it did serve as a firebrand to activists seeking justice against a law enforcement apparatus that seems to target, harass and brutalize people of color on a regular basis. Following Michael Brown's death, there was a series of other highly publicized instances of excessive force against black people, including the death of Eric Garner, who was choked to death for the crime of selling cigarettes without a permit; Philando Castille, who was shot and killed during a traffic stop for reaching for his wallet; and Tamir Rice, a 12 year old boy that was shot and killed for holding a toy gun in a public park. There are so many more that have garnered attention, and the stories continue to come out, day after day, as if nothing has been done to reign in police officers' use of violence against black people. Just this month, Dashawn McGrier was brutally beaten in Baltimore by a black police officer, proving that even black cops target black men with violence.

There is a real problem in this country between the black community and the law enforcement community, and it doesn't seem to be getting addressed as it should be. As shocking as all this bloodshed is, it is not new - and it is not surprising. This acrimony has been brewing for decades, and it will continue to fester until we address the underlying causes. There is not just one factor responsible for the strained relationship between blacks and police, but they are recognizable, and hopefully, with a little effort, surmountable. But it must start with the acknowledgement that, yes, there is a problem. And one of the primary drivers in this vicious cycle is the War on Drugs.

In the early part of the 20th century, there were practically no regulations on any drugs. In fact, many popular, over-the-counter medicines contained heroin and cocaine. It wasn't until 1914 that the federal government began restricting the sale of narcotics, with the passage of the Harrison Tax Act. By 1937, the FBI had cut its teeth on Depression-era gangsters and achieved some level of national prestige. Prohibition had ended, and meaningful federal health regulation was about to come about under the Food, Drug, and Cosmetics Act of 1938. The Federal Bureau of Narcotics, operating under the U.S. Treasury Department, had come into existence in 1930 under the leadership of Harry Anslinger, who is single-handedly responsible for much of the hysteria surrounding drugs and drug users that persists to this day.

And into this new national enforcement framework came the Marihuana Tax Act of 1937, which attempted to tax marijuana into oblivion. Marijuana had not been shown to be dangerous, but the perception that it might be a "gateway drug" for heroin users--and its alleged popularity among Mexican-American immigrants--made it an easy target.

General Dwight D. Eisenhower was elected president in 1952 by an electoral landslide based largely on his leadership during World War II. But it was his administration, as much as any other, that also defined the parameters of the War on Drugs. Not that it did so alone. The Boggs Act of 1951 had already established mandatory minimum federal sentences for possession of marijuana, cocaine, and opiates, and a committee led by Senator Price Daniel (D-TX) called that the federal penalties be increased further, as they were with the Narcotic Control Act of 1956. But it was Eisenhower's establishment of the U.S. Interdepartmental Committee on Narcotics, in 1954, in which a sitting president first literally called for a war on drugs.

In the period between the 1930s and 1970s, marijuana was considered a "Mexican drug." The proposal to enact a marijuana ban during the 1930s was wrapped up in racist anti-Mexican rhetoric. The Nixon administration closed the borders, trying to block the import of marijuana from Mexico. Operation Intercept imposed strict, punitive searches of traffic on the U.S.-Mexican border. The civil liberties implications of this policy are obvious, and it turned out to be a foreign policy disaster, due in part to the violence it caused in Mexico over the coming decades.

With passage of the Comprehensive Drug Abuse Prevention and Control Act of 1970, the federal government took a more active role in drug enforcement and drug abuse prevention. Nixon, who called drug abuse "public enemy number one" in a 1971 speech, emphasized treatment at first and used his administration's clout to push for the treatment of drug addicts, particularly heroin addicts. Nixon also targeted the trendy, psychedelic image of illegal drugs, asking celebrities such as Elvis Presley (shown left) to

113

help him send the message that drug abuse is unacceptable. Seven years later, Presley himself fell to drug abuse; toxicologists found as many as fourteen legally prescribed drugs, including narcotics, in his system at the time of his death.

Before the 1970s, drug abuse was seen by policymakers primarily as a social disease that could be addressed with treatment. After the 1970s, drug abuse was seen by policymakers primarily as a law enforcement problem that could be addressed with aggressive criminal justice policies. The addition of the Drug Enforcement Administration (DEA) to the federal law enforcement apparatus in 1973 was a significant step in the direction of a criminal justice approach to drug enforcement. If the federal reforms of the Comprehensive Drug Abuse Prevention and Control Act of 1970 represented the formal declaration of the War on Drugs, the Drug Enforcement Administration became its foot soldiers.

This isn't to say that law enforcement was the only component of the federal War on Drugs. As drug use among children became more of a national issue, Nancy Reagan toured elementary schools warning students about the danger of illegal drug use. When one fourth-grader at Longfellow Elementary School in Oakland, California asked Mrs. Reagan what she should do if approached by someone offering drugs, Reagan responded: "Just say no." The slogan, and Nancy Reagan's activism on the issue, became central to the administration's anti-drug message. It is not insignificant that the policy also came with political benefits. By portraying drugs as a threat to children, the administration was able to pursue more aggressive federal anti-drug legislation.

Powdered cocaine was the champagne of drugs. It was associated more often with white yuppies than other drugs were in the public imagination, while heroin was associated more often with African Americans, and marijuana with Latinos. Then along came crack, cocaine processed into little rocks at a price non-yuppies could afford. Newspapers printed breathless accounts of black urban "crack fiends" and the drug of rock stars suddenly grew more sinister to white middle America. Congress and the Reagan administration responded with the Anti-drug Act of 1986, which established a 100:1 ratio for mandatory minimums associated with crack cocaine. It would take 5,000 grams of powdered "yuppie" cocaine to land you in prison for a minimum 10 years--but only 50 grams of crack. And it is no secret that this policy fell much more significantly upon poor, black people.

In recent decades, the U.S. death penalty has been reserved for offenses that involve the taking of another person's life. The U.S. Supreme Court's ruling in Coker v. Georgia (1977) banned capital punishment as a penalty in cases of rape, and while the federal death penalty can be applied in cases of treason or espionage, nobody has been executed for either offense since the electrocution of Julius and Ethel Rosenberg in 1953. So when Senator Joe Biden's 1994 Omnibus Crime Bill, which was enthusiastically endorsed and signed into law by then-President Bill Clinton, included a provision allowing for the federal execution of drug kingpins, it indicated that the War on Drugs had ultimately reached such a level that drug-related offenses were regarded by the federal government as equivalent to, or worse than, murder and treason.

And make no mistake, this metaphorical "War" has indeed become an actual war, one that is waged in the streets of American cities, targeting American citizens as the enemies. Hundreds of innocent people have been killed as "collateral damage" in drug law enforcement activities. People like Kathryn Johnston, a 92-year-old woman whose house was erroneously raided by narcotics officers, was shot to death in a rain of bullets in her own home in 2006; Jonathan Ayers in 2009, a reverend who gave some money to a known drug addict and was then followed by police and shot dead; Rodolpho Cardenas in 2004, who police mistook for another person, was shot in the back and killed; Mario Paz in 1999, who was shot in the back in his own home when 20 officers conducted a 'no-knock' raid in the wrong house. These are just a few of the more heinous examples of the brutal failure of the War on Drugs. There are many, many more. And besides these obvious failures, hundreds of thousands of people have been thrown in prison - often with oppressive, unconscionably long sentences - for simple possession of drugs, losing their jobs, and often plunging their families into poverty. High crime areas, which are often predominantly black neighborhoods, are by far the most frequent battlegrounds in this protracted and expensive war. And the perpetual combat engaged in by law enforcement has led to the militarization of police departments around the country, which, as can be easily imagined, has only made matters worse.

The Department of Justice's Edward Byrne Memorial Justice Assistance Grant Program, and the Department of Defense's 1033 program, among others, have armed local law enforcement agencies with military and para-military equipment. Armored Personnel Carriers, flashbang grenades, and assault rifles, combined with aggressive training and tactics, have made police officers into combatants in a war, instead of public servants on our city streets. In fact, in many instances police officers are encouraged through their training to adopt a "warrior" mentality, and to "think of the people they are supposed to serve as enemies."

Special Weapons and Tactics (SWAT) teams, were originally adopted to handle emergency situations, such as hostage crises. However, today nearly 2/3 of SWAT deployments involve simple drug raids. They serve search warrants on the suspicion that someone may be in possession of drugs, often a small amount. These para-military SWAT teams break down doors in the middle of the night, with battering rams, toss a couple grenades into the house to blind and deafen the occupants, and enter, full assault style, to serve a search warrant. As should be expected, there is a greatly increased risk of violence in these raids, which are violent events in themselves.

Many police officers are honest, hard-working men and women. They perform heroic acts, and place themselves willingly in danger. But even these good officers are trained, armed and ordered to conduct aggressive, "proactive" policing, especially in "high crime" areas that are often neighborhoods of color. Police officers are sent into these areas to look for a fight, and to engage the public as enemy combatants. Is it any wonder that there are so many police shootings, when they are whipped into a frenzy and conditioned to be on high-alert at every moment?

And this increase in police aggression has led,

quite visibly, to mass incarceration of people of color. Not only are large numbers of African Americans incarcerated, African Americans are incarcerated at percentages that exceed any legitimate law enforcement interest and which negatively impact the African American community. While African Americans only comprise 12% of the U.S. population, they represent nearly half of those incarcerated in state and federal prisons. In fact, on average, African American males are approximately 8 times more likely to be incarcerated than white males. For some age groups, the racial disparities are even worse. For young men between the ages of 25 and 29, African Americans are closer to 10 times more likely to be incarcerated than whites.

It has been suggested, by people smarter than me, that the mass incarceration of African Americans is a direct consequence of the drug war. As one commentator has stated, 'Drug arrests are a principal reason that the proportions of [B]lacks in prison and more generally under criminal justice system control have risen rapidly in recent years.' Institutional racism is, of course, a strong component in this struggle between blacks and the criminal justice system, but even that factor is made easier, and more deadly, by the overly aggressive tactics involved in drug law enforcement. It allows officers to approach black men with the presumption that they are dealing with a dangerous criminal, even without any evidence to support such a presumption. The lingering portrait of the black "crack fiends" of the 1990's, and the violent image of black men that has been circulating through the public discourse since at least the 1970's, has made the unfair and disproportionate targeting of blacks by law enforcement easier still. But I firmly believe that if the War on Drugs finally enters a long-overdue cease-fire, we will at least begin to see the loosening of some of the tension between these two groups. And if even a fraction of the money - billions upon billions of dollars - that is wasted on the failed drug crusade is diverted to community programs and rehabilitation services, we may even begin to see a society-wide reduction in crime, poverty and conflict. Even if my predictions aren't exactly accurate, isn't it worth a try?

XIV.
Weed the People

Another blow was dealt to reasonable and rational drug policy in 2018 when the Drug Enforcement Administration (DEA) declined to re-schedule marijuana, choosing instead to keep the substance on the most restrictive schedule (Schedule I). In so doing, they are claiming, once again, that marijuana has a high potential for abuse, and no known medical value. Of course, both of these determinations are completely contrary to ALL the evidence we have available to us, but you know... science.

I didn't really expect the DEA to vote against its own interests and willingly remove one of the reasons for its own continued existence from its own continued oversight. But I am again baffled at the blatant refusal to acknowledge the will of the people, the weight of the scientific evidence, and the patent falsity of the claims that placed marijuana on Schedule I in the first place. At least come up with a different dirty lie. Earn your billions of dollars by at least trying to mislead us in a new way.

Marijuana should be legalized and regulated and taxed just like any other over the counter medication - or legal intoxicant. Indeed, study after study finds that marijuana is safer than alcohol and tobacco by extremely large margins. Studies also prove that marijuana is even safer than aspirin, Tylenol, or Advil. In fact, from a pure lethality standpoint, almost everything you put in your body is more toxic than marijuana. 50,000 Americans die every year as a direct result of alcohol; over 400,000 Americans die as a result of cigarettes; and over 1,000 people die each year from acetaminophen (Tylenol). A growing handful people have overdosed and died from caffeine. Hell, there have even been numerous deaths by so-called "water intoxication" - death from drinking too much water! You know how many deaths have been directly attributed to marijuana? Zero. In all of recorded history.

Marijuana usage dates back thousands of years. There is evidence of marijuana inhalation in ancient China dating back to 2700 B.C., where it was believed to be used in spiritual rituals and/or for medicinal purposes. Ancient Egyptians smoked marijuana, as well as making wide use of hemp, which is cultivated from the same plant as marijuana. There is even some viable research to suggest that Jesus Christ himself was a pot smoker, and that he may have used marijuana for ritual and healing purposes.

Indeed, the U.S.'s own history has strong ties to hemp and marijuana use, as even George Washington was an avid supporter and harvester of hemp, and Abraham Lincoln was said to enjoy a hemp pipe from time to time. It is even believed that drafts of the Declaration of Independence and the Constitution were written on Dutch hemp paper (although the final copies of each were written on parchment, not hemp, as some people erroneous believe).

It wasn't until the 20th century that governments around the world began efforts at prohibition of marijuana. There are many theories as to why marijuana was targeted. Some claim that the paper companies were behind it, because they feared that hemp paper could be produced cheaper - and work better - than wood pulp paper, putting them out of business. Some believe that alcohol producers were worried that marijuana would lower the demand for alcohol. And others believe that William Randolph Hearst, the legendary newspaper mogul, was behind the whole thing, as he certainly used his newspapers to spread false propaganda nationwide. Whether or not there was some mysterious dark co-conspirator in the push to criminalize marijuana, we do know that it was based on pure nonsense.

It was actually Harry Anslinger that led the campaign to criminalize marijuana and marijuana users. Anslinger was the head of the newly-formed Federal Bureau of Narcotics in 1930 and advocated furiously for the prohibition of marijuana. Anslinger believed that marijuana use caused violent crime, and caused people to act irrationally and become overly sexual. Of course these beliefs were not based on any actual evidence, but under his command, the FBN produced numerous propaganda films and materials designed to "educate" the public about these made-up problems. Perhaps the most well-known example of anti-marijuana propaganda was the 1936 film "Reefer Madness," which saw its main characters' lives torn apart by marijuana addiction. While not produced by Anslinger or the FBN, Reefer Madness was clearly a product of the hysteria and misinformation distributed by the government as part of Anslinger's quest.

Anslinger's crusade culminated in the Marijuana Tax Act of 1937, which made possession and transfer of marijuana illegal under Federal law. The Act was passed based on poorly-attended hearings, and questionable studies. In fact, in 1944, the LaGuardia Commission, formed by then-Mayor of New York City, Fiorello LaGuardia, issued a report contradicting earlier reports of violence, madness or overt sexuality., and advised against prohibition. And when Richard Nixon proposed to place marijuana on the newly-formed Controlled Substance Act schedule in the early 1970's, he also ordered a commission to examine the effects of marijuana legislation, and that commission also advised against prohibition. Of course, just as in 1944, the government ignored the Commission's opinion.

Marijuana was placed on Schedule I, the most restrictive, which includes illicit drugs such as heroin, LSD, and PCP ("Angel Dust"). Under *21 U.S.C. § 812*, drugs must meet three criteria in order to be placed in Schedule I:

1	The drug or other substance has a high potential for abuse.

2	The drug or other substance has no currently accepted medical use in treatment in the United States.

3	There is a lack of accepted safety for use of the drug or other substance under medical supervision.

There is strong evidence that marijuana fails to meet even the very first criterion. Studies show that marijuana is not physically addictive at all, and that even though some psychological dependence is observed, it is far lower than most other illegal and legal substances. Caffeine, nicotine and alcohol all have much higher addictive properties than pot. Repeated lab studies show that mice will not self-administer marijuana, a key indicator of addictiveness.

124

Even among frequent smokers, marijuana dependence is extremely low. Simply put, marijuana, if anything, has an extraordinarily LOW potential for abuse.

Furthermore, marijuana has been legalized for medical use in 25 states. There are currently about 150,000 patients that are regularly prescribed marijuana in those states. Over 2,500 doctors have recommended marijuana to patients. There are countless case studies confirming the health benefits of marijuana in the treatment of numerous conditions, including macular degeneration, AIDS and Cancer treatments, and treatment for chronic pain. There are dozens of national and international organizations, including the American Medical Association (AMA) and National Institutes of Health (NIH) that have issued statements in favor of medical marijuana. In other words, it is almost impossible to make the argument that marijuana has "no currently accepted medical use in treatment..."

And finally, as I stated previously, there is not one recorded death in all of human history attributed to marijuana toxicity. The amount of marijuana that could theoretically result in overdose and kill a human is absolutely impossible to actually ingest - something like the equivalent of 20,000 marijuana cigarettes. Indeed, you would likely die from smoke inhalation long before you overdosed on the actual marijuana. So it would seem that just about ANY dose of marijuana would be safe, with or without medical supervision.

Despite the evidence that marijuana absolutely doesn't belong on Schedule I, it continues to sit there. Since 1972, there have been tireless efforts to convince the DEA to remove marijuana from the Controlled

125

Substances Act, or to at least re-schedule it. All of the arguments made by lawmakers in support of continued prohibition have been thoroughly debunked. They claimed that it was a "gateway drug," that it was highly addictive, that it caused an increase in criminal behavior, or that it led to long-term brain damage, among many other societal and moral concerns. None of these claims is supported by a shred of evidence, and much evidence has been produced to refute them all. Yet again, marijuana remains on Schedule I, where it is presumed to be more dangerous than cocaine, methamphetamine, and opium (all Schedule II drugs).

In 2016, 25 states have now legalized marijuana for medical use, and 4 states plus the District of Columbia have effectively legalized it for recreational use. Medical and/or Recreational use is on the ballot in numerous other states, and the trend of legalization is expected to continue sweeping the nation. Public opinion polls show that a frank majority (63%) of Americans favor legalization, with almost 90% favoring decriminalization of some sort. Even so, every year more than 800,000 people are arrested for marijuana, most of them for just simple possession. We spend billions of dollars each year on marijuana law enforcement in this country, and send thousands of people to prison for often unconscionable sentences. Countless lives have been ruined - or made significantly more challenging - because of marijuana law enforcement.

Why do we continue to prosecute people for possessing pot? Well, in declining again to re-schedule (or de-schedule) marijuana, the DEA stated that, "the known risks of marijuana use have not been shown to be outweighed by specific benefits in well-controlled clinical trials that scientifically evaluate safety and efficacy." What risks?! The risk of eating an entire bag of Doritos while watching Scooby-Doo re-runs? They have never pointed to any risks that haven't already been falsified. The risk of dependence is extremely low, the risk of respiratory illness has been disproven, the risk of cancer is practically non-existent (in fact marijuana may be prophylactic of some forms of cancer), and the risk of overdose is imaginary. While there may be an increased risk of accidents by marijuana-intoxicated motorists, alcohol-intoxicated motorists are about 6 to 10 times more accident-prone. And there is a risk of short-term memory loss, but it is only temporary - usually only persisting while the user is under the effects of marijuana.

At any rate, there is no valid reason to continue the prohibition of marijuana. In fact, there was never a reason to prohibit it. The government decided to criminalize it based on nothing but speculation and uninformed opinion. Now they claim that the burden is on us to prove that it shouldn't be criminalized. *That's not how democracy works!* Government doesn't get to arbitrarily make things illegal and then make the people prove that they shouldn't be illegal. The government has the burden of proof to show why something should be illegal in the first place. They cannot meet that burden by simply stating that there *may* be risks that haven't been *specifically proven* to be outweighed by various benefits.

And so what if there are risks? There aren't, but what if there were? Everything carries with it some level of risk. Eating hamburgers increases risk of high cholesterol, high blood pressure, and a host of other health problems. Smoking cigarettes increases risks of cancer and numerous other serious and fatal diseases and illnesses. Drinking alcohol leads to cirrhosis, hepatitis, and many other terrible health disorders. Use of over-the-counter pain relievers lead to liver problems. Caffeine intake can lead to accidental overdose, toxicity and even death. But all of these substances are readily available without a prescription, and no amount of either will land you in jail. But because some ignorant fear-mongers from three-quarters of a century ago believed that marijuana use would lead to violent predators and sexual orgies, we are still stuck trying to prove that this natural substance shouldn't be used to send otherwise decent people to prison. As I've said before, it is not only bad policy to criminalize ingestion of a damn plant, it is absolutely immoral. And our government is not only engaging in immoral, bad policy in perpetuating this asinine enforcement regime, it is intentionally ignoring a clear majority of the people it's supposed to represent.

XV.
Kratom Kraze

Here we go again. Coming on the heels of the DEA's announcement that they would be completely disregarding scientists, doctors, lawmakers, and the general public who pays their bloated salaries in refusing to re-schedule marijuana, they now are placing another 100% natural, safe, and therapeutic plant on Schedule I. Mitragyna Speciosa, known colloquially as Kratom in the U.S., is a tropical deciduous tree in the same family as coffee, and which is indigenous (that means it grows all on its own, without any dirty drug kingpins' involvement) in Thailand. Mitragyna has been used as an herbal supplement in Thailand and other parts of the world for thousands of years, to help with pain and exhaustion, and is generally seen as a safe and uncontroversial substance.

So what's all the fuss? Well, apparently, here in the U.S. it has come to the attention of the DEA (via their corporate-pharmaceutical overlords) that chronic pain patients and others who are addicted to opioids (you know, legal drugs) have been using mitragyna to help alleviate withdrawal symptoms from opiate use. You see, mitragyna has a similar chemical profile as opium, targeting the μ-opioid receptors in the brain, yet has side effects that are far less potent than morphine or hydrocodone. This safer alternative has the potential to reverse a potentially deadly painkiller addiction, with fewer side effects, less risk of addiction, and pretty much no chance of death.

129

Use and abuse of prescription painkillers, such as hyrdrocodone, oxycontin and morphine, is epidemic in the U.S. Every year approximately 20,000 people are killed by accidental overdose from these legal substances. In addition to the deaths, many thousands of people see their lives spiral out of control due to painkiller addiction, losing jobs, alienating family, and struggling just to survive long enough to get one more refill. And when they can't get that refill, due to some other new arbitrary DEA pronouncement which prevents their treating physician from treating them, desperate addicts often turn to illicit drugs for relief. Usually heroin is substituted for painkillers, assuming the poor drug-addled buyer cant find any prescription pills on the black market, which itself is associated with almost 10,000 additional overdose deaths per year. But now there is a potentially viable and safe alternative to this wretched and vicious cycle in the form of plant that is closely related to coffee, but the DEA wants to deny them that relief. Stated differently, people who are trying to kick a life-destroying opiate habit by using a natural plant that is 100's of times safer than opiates are now going to be arrested, prosecuted and imprisoned in the same fashion as PCP and heroin users.

Apparently, the DEA has expressed concerns about people "using Kratom as an alternative to opiates." Like its a bad thing. Oh, I know, because some people will probably use Kratom *recreationally*, it must be bad, right? Because god knows anything that makes poor people feel a little better about themselves must be eradicated immediately. To illustrate this twisted logic, there was a time when Thailand government officials sought to outlaw mitragynine in Thailand, despite the overwhelming opposition from leaders, scientists and citizens. In their zeal to rid Thailand of this indigenous plant (remember, that means it grows naturally without any human assistance) they actually resorted to burning entire forests down - which included pristine rainforests! Talk about throwing the baby out with the bathwater. Happily, Thailand has wised up a bit since then by moving toward decriminalization in recent years. It is also noteworthy that mitragynine is not listed on any of the Schedules of the United Nations Drug Conventions, and is sparsely regulated in other areas of the world.

But that won't stop our mostly useless DEA from outlawing it here in the good ol' US of A. Using the antiquated language in the Controlled Substances Act as a panacea, they claim that "kratom has a high potential for abuse, has no currently accepted medical use in treatment in the United States, and has a lack of accepted safety for use under medical supervision." And that makes it wicked. Except that it doesn't. Donuts have a high potential for abuse, contribute heavily to obesity and heart disease, and have pretty much no conceivable medical use that I'm aware of. But the world's leader in obesity rates still has Krispy Kreme Donut shops dotted across the landscape every couple of miles.

Look, drugs aren't good for you. Things that affect our brain chemistry, either to help alleviate pain, counter fatigue, or just to feel good usually come at a price. Take nicotine or caffeine as an example - both of which are quite toxic and deadly at high doses, and both of which are extremely addictive. Or alcohol, which Americans love to pour down their throats as a part of daily life - which is directly related to more than 80,000 deaths every year. And don't forget about aspirin, acetaminophen and ibuprofen - which are also linked to numerous health issues and hundreds of deaths per year. But see, grownups get to make decisions about whether to use or abuse any of those substances without any interference from the long arm of the law. And that's the way it should be. But as it stands, we have a soulless, unaccountable governmental agency that has now decided *for* us that kratom - which has been responsible for approximately zero known deaths in human history - is off limits.

This may once again be an ugly example of some ideologue with a high Government Service rank attempting to legislate morality against the will of the people. Or, more likely, and just as uglily, it is an example of some corporate bribe-taker earning the dark contributions he receives from the pharmaceutical industry, which is intently opposed to any sort of alternative medicine that may chip away at profits. Either way, how much longer are We the People going to allow our government - a government that is supposed to govern by the *consent* of We the People - to dictate our personal lives against our will? I've never tried kratom. But I would like to think that if I was ever in a situation of opiate withdrawal - which people face every day - I could make a grownup decision to give it a try to avoid the living hell on Earth that often results from painkiller abuse. All grownups should have the option to make such a decision, regardless of its effect on corporate profit margins.

CHAPTER SIX
Prison & Sentencing Reform

"Remember those in prison as if you were their fellow prisoners, and those who are mistreated as if you yourselves were suffering."

- Hebrews 13:3

XVI.
Habitual Inequality

I have noticed over the course of my legal career that criminal defendants with money, or supportive families with money, fare better than those who are poor. We see it play out in several distinct ways within the criminal justice system. It has been pointed out how poor people pay astronomically higher fines and fees in traffic and misdemeanor courts, such as Municipal Courts. People with money get a traffic ticket, or some other minor municipal offense, like Disturbing the Peace, or Public Intoxication, and they simply pay the fine with a single check. These monied offenders are then off the hook, living footloose and fancy free. However, people without money - poor people - often cannot afford to pay the fine, and they have to be placed on some type of payment plan, almost always with an additional fee on top of the fine. If these people cannot make the payment, they may incur late fee penalties, of even contempt of court fines. John Oliver recently discussed this topic, highlighting a particular case - which is more common than you might think - where a person began with a $100 ticket, and ended up paying over $1,400!

We have also seen some discussion lately about the inequality when it comes to pre-trial offenders posting bail to get out of jail. Bail is set in practically every case, with few special exceptions. However, again, while people with money can post bail - even on serious charges - poor people often have much more difficulty - even on minor crimes. As it stands, it is not uncommon for a wealthy, white man charged with rape or murder, to post bail without spending even a few days in jail, while a poor, black man sits in jail for months on a minor marijuana charge simply because he couldn't afford the $150 required by the bondsman to post bail. In fact, last year the U.S. Justice Department actually acknowledged this problem, generating a memo that said "[b]ail practices that incarcerate indigent individuals before trial solely because of their inability to pay for their release violate the Fourteenth Amendment." Several high profile cases have since made progress toward evening that playing field, though there is still a long way to go.

More and more lately, I have also noticed another wealth-dependent privilege contained in the Multiple Offender statutes. These are laws that add additional and increased penalties for repeat offenders. Most states have a broad Habitual Offender statute that applies to all felony offenses and offenders. For example, a person with a prior burglary conviction will get a longer sentence on his 2nd burglary conviction pursuant to these Habitual Offender statutes. In Louisiana, 2nd and 3rd offenses generally carry up to double the maximum sentence for a first offense, while 4th time offenders face mandatory minimum 20 years in prison up to a maximum of life without parole - even for relatively minor drug offenses, such that a person with 3 prior convictions for simple possession of cocaine - or even non-narcotic prescription medication - can be locked up for life on a fourth offense.

There are also crime-specific multiple offender statutes, such as multiple offenses for Driving While Intoxicated (DWI). DWI is, in many states, referred to as an "enhanceable misdemeanor," meaning that the penalties vary depending on the number of previous DWI convictions. Again, in Louisiana, while DWI first and second offense are misdemeanors with a maximum of 6 months in jail, a fourth offense carries a minimum of 10 years up to a maximum of 20 years at hard labor.

While I am generally opposed to oppressive habitual offender sentencing schemes, I understand the reasoning behind them. As long as they aren't abused, and they offer judicial discretion to account for special circumstances, I don't generally have a strong objection. However, the way it is implemented in many places today is too strict, not taking the individual facts of the case into account, and essentially punishing petty thieves, or petty drug offenders, with the same degree of punishment as serious, violent offenders, such as murderers and rapists.

And, of course, there is a certain amount of inequality built into the statutes. Most habitual offender statutes will offer a "cleansing" period for prior convictions, only allowing the prosecutor to use convictions less than ten years old, for example. But that doesn't mean they can't still use older convictions, as long as there was a "linking" conviction less than ten years prior to the current charge. For instance, if you were charged in 2017 with a felony, and you had a prior felony conviction in 2008, and another in 1999, and another in 1990, they could charge you as a fourth-time felony offender, since each of the prior convictions is less than 10 years older than the next one. However, if you were charged in 2017 and your prior convictions were in 2006, 2005, and 2004, you could still be a first time offender, since the most recent one was more than ten years ago.

There's a catch - and this is where is gets really unfair - the time period for "cleansing" your record does not start to run until the end of your sentence on the prior conviction, and - wait for it - ***payment of all fines and fees***. So here we go again, a system where you get a faster cleansing period just by having more money. So a rich guy could get convicted of a felony in 2007, get 6 months probation and a $1,000 fine, and would be completely cleansed by mid-2017, free to commit another consequence-free felony. However, a poor guy could get the same sentence, yet not be able to pay the fine up front, and have to go on a payment plan, and pay additional fees, and sometimes contempt of court fees if he misses a payment, or could lose his job and stop paying altogether, and he could still be technically "on probation" for years. During that entire time - until the last dollar is paid - the clock is stopped on his cleansing period.

It is well settled in our law that a person cannot be punished for their inability to pay fines and fees. In the case of an indigent defendant it is impermissible to impose a prison term in lieu of fine payment that would result in the defendant's serving a longer term than the maximum for the offense, *Williams v. Illinois*, 399 U.S. 235, 90 S.Ct. 2018, 26 L.Ed.2d 586 (1970). It is likewise impermissible to imprison an indigent defendant for failure to pay a fine for a crime punishable by fines only, *Tate v. Short*, 401 U.S. 395, 91 S.Ct. 668, 28 L.Ed.2d 130 (1971). Most importantly, it is a constitutional violation to revoke a person's probation, and increase their punishment, because the defendant could not pay his fine without determining that he had not made sufficient bona fide efforts to pay or that adequate alternative forms of punishment did not exist. *Bearden v. Georgia,* 461 U.S. 660, 103 S.Ct. 2064, 76 L.Ed.2d 221 (1983). Unfortunately, this framework has not yet been applied to the application of habitual offender statutes.

I have personally seen people who are charged with a 2nd offense DWI 25 years after a prior DWI, even though the cleansing period is 10 years, because they didn't - or couldn't - pay all the fines and fees they owed for the previous case. Or perhaps even worse, I had a client with a prior felony theft charge from 2003 for which he received a 1 year sentence, plus a fine. He successfully completed his probation, and paid all of his fines. However, because there was some nominal court cost and/or administrative fee not paid in full, the record was not marked "closed" for several additional years. When he was arrested again in 2016, because that case was not officially closed until 2007, he was charged as a habitual offender, when again, the cleansing period is ten (10) years.

I am not here advocating for the abolishment of habitual offender laws. I am not advocating for the "right" of criminals to have an easier time avoiding enhanced sentences for recidivism. I do have some pretty fundamental objections to the way most habitual offender statutes are written, but I will save those arguments for another article. At this time, I am specifically opposed to the inequity written into these laws, allowing people with money to enjoy less severe consequences than those without money. A law is not necessarily unfair if it invokes harsh consequences, but it is absolutely unfair if those consequences affect different people differently based solely on their ability to pay money. That is a violation of the Equal

Protection clause of the 14th Amendment, and should
be addressed. I'll hold my breath while I'm waiting.

XVII.
Profiting From Injustice

As a criminal defense lawyer, I have seen the inside of the justice system up close, and am well versed in the lies, misconceptions, inefficiencies and abuses that plague that system. And I have seen my share of young, non-violent offenders slapped with oppressive prison sentences for relatively minor crimes. Thankfully, there seems to be a new movement emerging in many parts of the country to reform the criminal justice system, but rest assured that progress will be slow, and opponents will invariably present a compelling case against reform based on inaccurate information and fear mongering tactics. It is these detractors that keep an 18th century mob mentality ingrained in our culture -harkening back to the days of the Salem Witch Trials.

The particular trouble with reforming criminal justice, is the preconception that most people have about "criminals" in the first place. Proponents of reform have to break through a very hard and deeply ingrained prejudice to even engage in a meaningful conversation. And that is made more difficult by the fact that most people will simply tune out reform proponents before any real ground can be gained. Let the police do their jobs, let criminals pay for their crimes, and who cares if some criminals' rights are violated - they shouldn't have rights in the first place.

There is a psychological concept known as "Polarization of Opinion," and it is particularly relevant in a conversation about unpopular and/or emotionally charged public policy issues, like the reform of our criminal justice system. Basically, when people with opposing views interpret new information in a biased way, their views can move even further apart. This is called, more specifically, "attitude polarization".

This effect was demonstrated by two researchers, Charles Taber and Milton Lodge, who conducted a study using the emotionally charged topics of gun control and affirmative action. They measured the attitudes of their participants towards these issues before and after reading arguments on each side of the debate. Two groups of participants showed attitude polarization: those with strong prior opinions and those who were politically knowledgeable. In part of this study, participants chose which information sources to read, from a list prepared by the experimenters. For example they could read the National Rifle Association's and the Brady Anti-Handgun Coalition's arguments on gun control. Even when instructed to be even-handed, participants were more likely to read arguments that supported their existing attitudes than arguments that did not. This biased search for information correlated well with the polarization effect.

There is a similar effect known as the "backfire effect," first coined by Brendan Nyhan and Jason Reiflerwhich, which is a form of attitude polarization that works in reverse, so to speak. Participants demonstrating the backfire effect, when given evidence *against* their beliefs, tended to reject the evidence and believe in their preconceived point of view even more strongly.

These specific cognitive handicaps contribute

to the type of thinking that keeps people from appreciating the damage that is done to society by excessive law enforcement and over zealous prosecution and imprisonment. It is that same problem that makes the arguments of reform opponents resonate so loudly. People already have a prejudice against criminals, and thus anything that seeks to demonize criminals and build fear against reform, is very readily embraced by the masses. And any evidence that contradicts these strong beliefs is disregarded, discounted, or misinterpreted to strengthen those already-entrenched beliefs. Therefore, law enforcement advocates - and there are plenty of them given that law enforcement and imprisonment are both big businesses - can distort information, or simply make up lies, and no one questions them. Crime bad - prison good.

Let's start with some baseline statistics to establish just how big our crime and punishment business is. First, because America loves superlatives, it is no surprise that we are number 1 in the incarceration race. That's right, not only does the US lead the globe in incarceration rates, ie the number of people in prison as a percentage of our population, but we also boast the highest absolute number of citizens behind bars, even though we are not the most populous. The U.S. has less than 5% of the world's population, yet boasts almost 25% of the world's prison population. Currently, there are more than 2 million people in state and federal prisons in the U.S., and another half million in local jails. Besides those actually incarcerated, there are another 5 million or so on probation and parole. That's over 7 million people under correctional supervision in the U.S., which represents a whopping 2.9% of all adults in the country.

Between 1925 and 1970, the incarceration rate remained at approximately the same level, with slight fluctuations in the intervening years. However, in the early 1970's, the rate began skyrocketing exponentially, and has since increased almost **500%**. What is fueling this rapid and unprecedented increase in the number of people in prison? Well, there is much to write about the multitude of causes, but the primary culprits are the war on drugs and militarization of police department along with the birth and rapid expansion of the prison-industrial complex.

Since the dawn of the nation, some form of cooperation existed between state and federal authorities and private industry. For much of modern history, there have been contracts between prisons and private vendors for specialty services such as food preparation, inmate transportation and medical services. However, in the 1980s, with the War on Drugs raging on, prison overcrowding became a serious issue, and there was a need for more space. The regrettable response to this "need," was the rise of the private prison industry.

In 1984, Corrections Corporation of America (CCA), became the first private company to take over an entire prison facility, in Hamilton County, Tennessee. The private prison business has now grown to be a $5 billion a year industry. CCA's profits have increased more than 500 percent. Since its inception in this burgeoning industry, CCA has been the subject of a plethora of lawsuits alleging rampant violence, understaffing, gang activity and contract fraud.

Recently, a dedicated journalist went undercover at a private prison in Louisiana - Winn Correctional, one of many owned by CCA. He did this because it became clear that private prisons are not at all transparent with reporters, often allowing them access to the prison only through carefully guided tours and monitored interviews with inmates. He noted that these prisons' records are often not subject to public access laws, a particularly sinister perquisite offered to these companies, allowing them to avoid the disclosure rules applicable to public corrections centers.

What was revealed by the journalist's four months as a CCA corrections officer was really not surprising, albeit a little disconcerting. For instance, the facilities were understaffed, and the employees were underpaid. As would be expected, the guards were relatively unprofessional, poorly trained, and reluctant to exhibit any initiative. If they saw two prisoners fighting, or stabbing each other, the guards were instructed to tell the inmates to stop. If the inmates didn't stop, the guards were instructed to just walk away. Breaking up a fight entails a level of risk that $9.00 an hour just doesn't cover. And violence by guards on prisoners is not only common, but applauded.

There is also rampant prisoner-on-prisoner violence, with very little supervision. The conditions are often filthy, and the prisoners are offered practically no enrichment programs, instead left to sit around all day doing nothing constructive, and often doing things that are patently un-constructive. One of the most obvious externalities of all this free time is the rate of sexual assault in CCA-run prisons. In Winn Correctional, the sexual abuse rate is almost double that of other state-run facilities. And the guards and staff do little to reverse that disturbing trend.

As unsettling as the poor conditions and lack of safety are in private prisons, there is potentially a more ominous endeavor engaged in by the private prison industry - establishing a renewable customer base. Private prisons are generally paid on a per prisoner basis, therefore the prison companies want to keep their cells full. They do this in a variety of ways. One way is to extend prison stays for its current customers, usually by way of taking away "good time" credits from inmates for minor rule infractions. Another way is through so-called "occupancy guarantees" that are contained within a large majority of the contracts CCA and other private prison companies enter into with state and federal agencies. These guarantee clauses require the government to provide a certain number of prisoners to the private prison at all times, failing which results in a penalty. One can imagine, I hope, that having quotas on prisoners has a very uncomfortable potential for abuse.

Perhaps one of the most disquieting examples of the potential for abuse in the for-profit prison system has become known as the "kids for cash" scandal. In 2008 in Wilkes-Barrre, Pennsylvania, Judges Mark Ciavarella and Michael Conahan, were convicted of accepting bribes from Mid-Atlantic Youth Services Corp, a private prison company which runs juvenile facilities. A representative of Mid-Atlantic was found to have paid the two judges $2.8 million in exchange for imposing harsh sentences on juveniles in order to increase the number of inmates at their facilities in the state. Approximately 2,000 children were sentenced to serve time at Mid-Atlantic prisons, many for petty crimes such as trespassing in vacant buildings and stealing DVDs from Wal-Mart in exchange for the bribes.

More subtly, though no less despicably, the private prison industry lobbies state and federal lawmakers for legislation that increases incarceration rates and lengths of sentences, such as habitual offender laws (often referred to as "three strike laws") that drastically increase a criminal defendant's prison term based on his previous criminal record. In my practice, I have seen, first hand, such oppressive sentencing regimes wreak terrible consequences, such as non-violent drug addicts being sentenced to 20 or 30 years, sometimes even life without parole, for relatively minor offenses.

Private prison companies are not solely, nor even primarily, the source of our mass incarceration problem, but they are a dark and ugly component of it. For the sake of profits, these facilities are poorly managed, unsafe, and unsanitary. These companies expend great effort to boost occupancy, by encouraging longer prison sentences, extending sentences for current inmates, and, at least occasionally, engaging in unethical practices such as bribery. All of which compromises civil liberties and basic human decency in the name of boosting revenue. Vermont Senator Bernie Sanders, who introduced the "Justice is Not For Sale Act" in 2015 attempting to prohibit the government from contracting with private companies, once stated:

"Keeping human beings in jail for long periods of time must no longer be an acceptable business model. . . We have got end the private prison racket in America."

And there is really no good argument to continue allowing this practice. It has proven to enable substandard confinement conditions and corruption, and the cost savings to the states is minimal, at best. In fact two studies found that the actual cost savings of contracting to private, unregulated facilities amounted to less than 15% over state-run and regulated facilities. And the conditions have proven to be far worse, with twice as many violent assaults and sexual abuse of inmates, both by other inmates and by prison personnel. There are simply some things in a civilized society that should not be privatized. Prisons should be one of those things. End the private prison industry now.

XVIII
Unconstitutionally Excessive:
A True Story of Excessive Sentencing

The Eighth Amendment to the U.S. Constitution proscribes the imposition of "cruel and unusual punishment" upon any person accused and convicted of a crime. While there is no clear and unambiguous definition of "cruel and unusual" contained within the Constitution, the judiciary has attempted to lay the foundation for any such analysis. For example, if a sentence results in the needless imposition of pain and suffering and is grossly disproportionate to the seriousness of the offense so as to shock the Court's sense of justice, the sentence is considered unconstitutionally excessive and violative of the prohibition against cruel, excessive, or unusual punishment. State v. Lobato,. "A sentence may be excessive either by length or because the circumstances warrant a less onerous sentencing alternative." State v. Webster. The Courts must examine whether a punishment is unconstitutionally excessive as to each particular case. State v. Sepulvado. A sentence may be unconstitutionally excessive even if it is within the statutory limit imposed by the legislature. If a sentence makes no "measurable contribution to acceptable goals of punishment" the trial judge has a duty to reduce such sentence to one which would not be constitutionally excessive. State v. Dorthey.

However, sometimes you get a case where all these pronouncements against excessive sentences are seemingly ignored. The following story is a harrowing journey by a client of mine, first as a public defender, and then as a private *pro bono* attorney, who faced a felony burglary charge in New Orleans, from his arraignment in 2010 to today, eight years later. While all of the facts and details I set forth are contained in the public record, and I am divulging no confidential information, I have, as a courtesy to all parties, changed the names of everyone involved.

On September 5, 2010, my client was arrested and charged with Simple Burglary of an Inhabited Dwelling, a second class felony. Allegedly, the home of one of the Assistant District Attorneys was burglarized on August 17, 2010. Through its investigation, the New Orleans Police Department developed another man - we'll call him Jackie - as a suspect. When Jackie was arrested and interrogated, he alleged that my client was involved in the burglary. Jackie was offered a plea deal, and he pled guilty as charged. Jackie was already a habitual offender, having been previously convicted of at least one prior felony, he admitted that he burglarized the ADA's home, and he also admitted that he committed at least four (4) other felonies as well. As charged, he was facing more than eighty (80) years in prison. Yet Jackie was offered a plea bargain, whereby he would be sentenced to six (6) years, and the State would refrain from filing a Multiple Bill against him. Thus, with good time, Jackie would serve only about 2 ½ years for committing four burglaries.

You see, luck was on Jackie's side. The lead investigator in the case - Detective Wall - was an old friend, and they had gone to school together. Detective Wall admitted that he did not want to see his old school chum in trouble. Unfortunately, Jackie had broken into an Assistant District Attorney's home. Someone had to go down for this one. As luck would have it, at the time Jackie was arrested, weeks after the burglary, he was riding in a vehicle with an older black guy, my client, who henceforth we will refer to as David.

Based on Jackie's statement that David was involved in the burglary, Jackie was offered the deal of a lifetime, and David was arrested and charged under La. R.S. 14:62.1. Based on his alleged criminal history, David was potentially facing a life sentence. The same district attorney's office that offered Jackie 6 years (eligible for parole in 2 ½), offered David 25 years, as a habitual offender, which would mean he would not be eligible for parole, and would essentially serve all 25 years. As a fifty year old man, this was tantamount to a life sentence.

This is important to show the fundamental unfairness in the way these two men were treated. Jackie was lucky indeed. Not only did he know the lead detective, it turns out that his family was good friends with the victim's family. And the victim was employed as an assistant District Attorney in New Orleans, under the same District Attorney that charged and prosecuted David in this matter. We attempted to alleviate some of the bias in this case by filing a Motion to Recuse the district attorney's office, based on a very glaring conflict of interest. The motion was denied, and the Orleans D.A.'s office prosecuted David through trial. And the fundamental unfairness did not stop there.

At trial, Jackie testified. Up to this point, the only evidence that could be offered against David was a grainy video from a gas station where the victim's debit has been used after the burglary, showing a black male in the vicinity of a white male – although the white male alone used the stolen debit card; and evidence that a black male, eventually identified as David in a photographic lineup, was with Jackie several days after the burglary, when he alone sold another item from the burglary.   No other evidence was offered implicating David in this crime, until Jackie testified.

Jackie first stated that he entered the apartment alone. He claimed that he rode to the apartment with David, but that he, himself, went into the apartment. After the State asked the Court to declare Jackie a hostile witness, he requested his own attorney. He then met with an attorney for approximately an hour. After he met with her, he changed his testimony to suggest that it was David that chose the location of the burglary, and that David was with him when he went inside. Interestingly, Jackie seemed unsure of anything unless he first reviewed a transcript of his recorded statement taken by Detective Wall. He testified that he was under the influence of narcotics, including heroin, at the time of the burglary, and that he only had a vague recollection of certain events of that night. He also stated that he was going through withdrawal symptoms at the time of his interview with Detective Wall. And finally, he stated that Detective Wall, his childhood friend, told him that if testified in the case, he could probably get a deal.

There was no other evidence presented in the case against David. No one, other than Jackie, was able to put him in that apartment on August 17, 2010. The grainy video may have shown David, but it certainly did not prove, beyond a reasonable doubt, that David was with Jackie at the time of the burglary. The testimony of another witness may have supported the argument that David was with Jackie days after the burglary, but certainly did not establish any connection between David and the burglary. The only evidence that arguably implicated David in the burglary was the self-serving testimony of Jackie, made after consulting with an attorney for an hour in the middle of trial, and made only after reviewing his own recorded statement several times.

Prior to trial, during jury selection, the State used ten of eleven peremptory challenges to strike black jurors. The defense objected and asserted a Batson challenge. The State then listed several clearly pretextual reasons for striking those jurors. The Court denied the *Batson* challenge, and the jury was sat with predominantly white jurors - 10 out of 12 - even though the venire was approximately 64% black. Furthermore, following the markedly unfair trial, the jury returned with a verdict that stated "Guilty of Attempted Simple Burglary of Inhabited Dwelling." However, the jury foreman had written the verdict on the front of the verdict form. The Judge suggested that the paperwork was wrong, and with very vague and confusing instructions, instructed the jury to return to the Jury Room and either re-do the paperwork or re-commence deliberations. The jury came back down in a very short time, this time writing the verdict on the back of the form. The jury had written "Guilty of Attempted Simple Burglary of Inhabited Dwelling" again, but then scratched it out and wrote "Guilty of Simple Burglary of Inhabited Dwelling." Clearly, the Judge improperly invaded the fact-finding process and refused to recognize a legal verdict, and David was greatly prejudiced as a result. Finally, the verdict reached by the jury was 10 votes to 2 - a non-unanimous verdict, which in Louisiana is still considered a legal verdict, even when the defendant is facing a potential life sentence. Only two states still support non-unanimous jury verdicts, and Oregon is set to change its law in the near future. And, guess what, the only two African American jurors on the panel voted against the verdict.

After trial, and several post-trial motions that were barely even considered by the presiding judge, David was sentenced to the maximum of 12 years at hard labor. Almost two full years later, the State finally filed a Habitual Offender bill against him, alleging him to be a fourth felony offender. Apparently, in 1989, David pled guilty to possession of narcotics; in 1994 he pled guilty to burglary of a parked car; and in 2004, he pled guilty to another minor narcotics charge. However, based on the Draconian sentencing structure in Louisiana, this non-violent record allowed the sentencing judge to sentence David to Life Without Parole - a sentence that is usually reserved for murder and aggravated rape. And again, without blinking an eye, the judge did just that, sending David to die at Angola prison.

This happened in 2014. We filed appeals as to both the conviction and the sentence. I was rather disappointed that the Court of Appeal took no notice of any of the Constitutional challenges we made regarding his unfair trial. But I usually am disappointed by what the Court of Appeal takes no notice of. We were almost out of options. We even had a local news outlet run a special segment on the story, trying to get some relief from such a crushing defeat.

Then, last year, the Court of Appeal finally ruled on the constitutionality of David's sentence. While they did not actually declare the sentence unconstitutional, they did say that the sentencing judge failed to conduct a meaningful hearing, and thus remanded the case to the district court for resentencing. We took advantage of this break. In the intervening years, the presiding judge had retired, and we had a fresh face to appeal to. We met with the district attorney once again and were finally able to iron out a deal whereby David would plead guilty as a second felony offender, with a sentence of 20 years. It sounds like a long time, however, thanks to a welcome change in the legislature just this past session, it meant that David would be eligible for parole after 25% of his sentence. He had already served over 7 years at the time. A few weeks ago, I heard that David had a parole hearing scheduled. I enthusiastically sent a letter to the parole board, campaigning for David's release.

I got the call last Friday, from David himself, that he was home. I had been in communication with his family throughout the past several years, but it was still a welcome surprise to wake up Friday morning to his voice. David spends much of his time now volunteering at the New Orleans mission, counseling homeless people and trying to give back something to the community. He is a changed man, and we hope he has a long happy life ahead of him, surrounded by friends and family.

While this story ultimately has a happy ending, the tragedy of it is that it happened in the first place.

And this kind of thing happens all too often. Here, there and everywhere around this country, people in the criminal justice system become victims of overzealous police work, politicized prosecutions, favoritism and bias, and, unfortunately, racism. Sentencing laws in this country are oppressive, and excessive, even for minor offenses. The War on Drugs has militarized police departments, making community policing more of a ground war with disadvantaged citizens. And the 'tough on crime' mentality that has developed over the past few decades has led America to the very top of the incarceration race, boasting not only the highest per capita prison population in the world, but also the highest absolute number of people behind bars. Our justice system needs a serious overhaul, and the way we look at and respond to crimes - especially non-violent ones - is outdated, antiquated and has got to change.

CHAPTER SEVEN
Criminal Justice Reform

""There is no greater tyranny than that which is perpetrated under the shield of the law and in the name of justice."

- Charles-Louis de Secondat,
baron de la Brède et de Montesquieu

XIX.
Capital Punishment and Mental Illness

The U.S. is one of only 36 nations worldwide (18%) that still carries out the death penalty. And we are currently in 5th place for the number of executions each year. We are only outdone by a handful of theocratic and/or totalitarian countries, such as Saudi Arabia, Iran and North Korea. Over half of the nations of the world (53%) have completely abolished the death penalty for all crimes, including virtually the entirety of Europe and South America. Another 26% of countries, while maintaining the death penalty in theory, either have a moratorium on executions or have not used capital punishment in at least ten (10) years. Indeed, even a majority of U.S states have abolished the death penalty, either explicitly or in practice. And perhaps more surprisingly, most death sentences carried out in recent years in the U.S. have been in a tiny handful of jurisdictions, mostly concentrated in the deep south.

The death penalty is, thankfully, falling out of favor around the world, and, finally, here in the U.S. Even in execution-happy Texas, we are seeing a drastic decline in death sentences being handed down. In 1999, Texas juries sentenced 48 people to death. In 2013 that number dropped to 9 death sentences. And in 2015, Texans only sentenced 2 people to die. It is also interesting to note that only 10 counties nationwide imposed 6 or more death sentences between 2010 and 2015, and only 2% of counties were responsible for 56% of the nation's population on death row.

It was recently reported that only 25 people were executed in America in 2018, continuing the downward trend we have seen with the executions in the U.S. Yet, even with the obvious change in public acceptance of capital punishment, and despite a growing body of knowledge about the failures, fallacies and inequities of the death penalty, our government and court system seem absolutely unwilling to put this outdated system to rest once and for all. While we have been on the right track for a number of years, it should still be unacceptable in today's world for any number of executions to be carried out, especially in an advanced, modern, and civilized nation.

I have numerous objections to capital punishment: it is expensive; it is ineffective as a deterrent; there is an unacceptable margin of error; and it is cruel, which should disqualify it under the 8th Amendment's prohibition against "cruel and unusual punishment." However, most important to me, is that the death penalty is antiquated, barbaric, and nothing more than state-sponsored murder. It is the killing of an unarmed person, when that person poses no immediate threat to any other person. It is murder. And perhaps worst of all, in a shocking percentage of cases, the condemned is suffering from mental illness at the time of the crime and/or at trial and/or at the time they are executed. All my ideological reasons for opposing the death penalty aside, the practice of executing mentally ill people should repel even the most pro-death proponent.

In March of 2015, the State of Missouri executed a man named Cecil Clay for the 1996 murder of a police officer. Cecil Clay was verifiably mentally deficient, having lost 20% of his brain's prefrontal cortex - the part of he brain that controls decision making - in a sawmill accident. He was diagnosed, long before his fatal encounter with police, as having "chronic brain syndrome", which caused his IQ to diminish to approximately 71. Three different doctors declared Cecil Clayton incompetent to be executed, but that didn't stop Missouri from killing him with a secret cocktail of deadly poison. I remember one of the things that I found so shocking was that Cecil Clayton, who was profoundly religious, believed that Jesus was going to spare him. Even as he was being walked down the "longest mile" to the execution chamber, he still insisted that Jesus was going to intervene to save his life. Needless to say, Christ did no such thing.

The following year, in April 12, 2016, the State of Georgie executed a man named Kenneth Fults. The condemned Fults had committed a fairly brutal murder of his neighbor. Incidentally (or not), his neighbor was a white girl - and he was neither. He was a black man, and in 1996 he committed a number of burglaries. During the course of his last burglary he shot his neighbor in the back of the head 5 times. He confessed to the murder, and he pled guilty at trial. After accepting responsibility, the jury sentenced him to death. 20 years later, his sentence was carried out via lethal injection of pentobarbital.

Kenneth Fults told police that he killed his neighbor while he was in a "dream-like state." He stated that he didn't mean to kill her - it was just an accident. Normally when someone shoots somebody else in the back of the head 5 times, I have a hard time

163

believing it was an accident. However, in the case of Kenneth Fults, I have a bit more credulity. You see, Kenneth Fults is - or was - intellectually disabled. He had a functional IQ of only 74, which is, in most classification tables, considered "well below average" or "borderline impaired or delayed," and put him in the lowest 1% of the population. In addition to his obvious mental deficiencies, Kenneth was also abused, neglected and bullied as a child. In other words, he had a substantial amount of mental and emotional baggage long before he committed the crimes which condemned him to death.

These people were executed, even though there are Supreme Court precedents that specifically prohibit carrying out the death penalty on mentally disabled people. In *Atkins v. Virginia* the Supreme Court of the United States ruled 6-3 that executing people with ***intellectual disabilities*** violates the Eighth Amendment's ban on cruel and unusual punishments. That decision was handed down in 2002. So shouldn't it have applied to prohibit Georgia and Missouri from executing those mentally impaired prisoners? Of course it ***should*** have, except that the Supreme Court's decision in *Atkins* failed to offer any definition, or even guidance, on what constitutes intellectual disability. The *Atkins* decision actually explicitly left that determination to the individual states.

It turns out, that the specific holding in *Atkins* applied to "mentally retarded" people, although mental retardation was likewise left to the States to interpret. For example, in Virginia, where *Atkins* was decided, they rely largely on the IQ of the accused to determine mental retardation. In Atkins' own case, in fact, he had been spared from the death penalty when the evidence suggested his IQ was only 56. However, later it was determined that his intellect had improved through the course of his legal proceedings, and that his IQ rose to above 70, which, under Virginia law, was no longer considered mentally retarded. The reviewing court opined that Atkins' previously low score was tainted by his use of drugs and alcohol, among other things. Thus, Atkins was once again scheduled to be executed, ignoring the fact that a 70 IQ is still considered borderline at best.

Don't worry, Atkins was ultimately spared - again. Following the court's decision to move forward with his execution, another judge raised allegations of prosecutorial misconduct and ultimately commuted his sentence to life in prison. So, as of the time of this writing, presumably Atkins is still alive, and is no longer on death row. But don't take this as a happy ending to this article. There have been many others who weren't as lucky as Atkins.

One such unlucky inmate was Warren Hill. Hill was sentenced to life in prison for murder in 1986. However, while he was in prison, he allegedly killed another inmate, and in 1991, for the murder of that inmate, Warren Hill was sentenced to die. There was strong evidence of Warren Hill's mental disability, including testimony from seven (7) mental health experts - all of the mental health experts that had ever examined him - that Warren Hill was mentally retarded. However, despite numerous stays of his execution by state and Federal courts, Warren Hill was executed in January, 2015. The problem is that in Georgia, which is free to set its own standards for determining intellectual disability, a defendant is required to prove mental retardation beyond a reasonable doubt. Unfortunately for people like Mr. Hill, mental health diagnoses are subject to a degree of uncertainty that is virtually impossible to overcome. The U.S. Delegation to the European Union, President Jimmy Carter and Rosalyn Carter, the American Bar Association, the Georgia NAACP, the ACLU and the Council of Europe all called for Warren Hill's execution to be stayed. None of it did any good.

In addition to the pronouncements in *Atkins* prohibiting the execution of intellectually disabled or mentally retarded individuals, the Supreme Court in <u>*Ford v. Wainwright*, 477, U.S. 399, (1986)</u> stated that defendants who were **insane** cannot be executed. Insanity is obviously different than intellectually disabled. An insane person may be found competent to proceed to trial, yet may assert a defense of "not guilty by reason of insanity" or "NGRI" for the seasoned trial lawyer. The first "insanity test" arose in 1843 with the case of M'Naughten, who was acquitted on grounds of insanity. In that case it was stated that in order for a defendant to be found not guilty by reason of insanity, he must show he suffers from a mental disease or defect that caused him to either 1) not know the nature and quality of the act he committed, or 2) not know that the act was wrong. The first prong of the test looks at cognitive capacity, ie did the mental disease/defect keep the defendant from knowing what he was doing, and the second prong at moral capacity, ie did the mental disease/defect keep the defendant from understanding the act was wrong.

This test has been adopted by most American States, but has been criticized recently for its failure to reflect modern psychiatric knowledge. Moreover,

166

there is no constitutionally minimum standard for the insanity defense and the U.S. Supreme Court has specifically upheld limited definitions, such as the one in Louisiana which exempts the offender's cognitive capacity as grounds for an insanity plea, as constitutional. <u>Clark v. Arizona</u>, 548 U.S. 735 (2006). Despite the public perception, an insanity defense is rarely used, only appearing in less than 1% of all criminal cases. Even then, an insanity defense is only successful 26% of the time in that small fraction of cases. An ACLU report shows that juries "frequently reject insanity defenses in capital cases despite strong evidence that the defendants are suffering from serious mental illnesses at the time of the crime." And not surprisingly, many defendants with rather obvious signs of mental illness are punished nonetheless.

Lastly, the Court in <u>Panetti v. Quarterman, 551 U.S. 930 (2007)</u>, reconfirmed that defendants could not be executed while they were found to be mentally *incompetent*, and during the duration of any such incompetence. Competence is yet a different standard, and can occur for any number of reasons. Sometimes mental illness prevents the offender from being competent, and other times a brain injury or trauma can render them incompetent. But competence is not necessarily permanent. In fact, when competency is raised, it is the job of forensic psychologists and psychiatrists to determine whether the defendant is competent, and whether, if incompetent, the defendant is capable of being restored to competence. Restoration services can include counseling and/or medication, and may be as simple as managing an offender's mental illness symptoms. If a person is found to be mentally retarded, or permanently insane, they may be found "irrestorably incompetent." If this finding takes place while the case is pending, the case may be stayed indefinitely, and the offender is often referred to a custodial psychiatric facility for treatment and assessment.

Competence is likewise not well-defined, and courts have a limited toolkit for probing this question. The Supreme Court stated in <u>*Dusky v. United States*, 362 U.S. 402, 402 (1960)</u> that a defendant is competent if "he has sufficient present ability to consult with his lawyer with a reasonable degree of rational understanding-and [if] he has a rational as well as factual understanding of the proceedings against him." However, because of the limited inquiry involved in a competency evaluation, an inmate who is found competent may still be insane or intellectually disabled, and, in fact, such a situation is far more common than most people think, and certainly far more common than courts and corrections officers are willing to admit. Thus, many "competent" people are found guilty, sentenced, and far too often executed, with serious mental health issues.

The primary problem with the system as it is, is that while we have these designations - intellectual disability, insanity, and competency - we have no general provision for defendants with mental illness. A person may have schizophrenia, bipolar disorder and manic depressive disorder, yet still be found competent, sane and not intellectually disabled. To be sure, many people with profound mental illnesses are quite intelligent, and would easily satisfy the *Dusky* criteria for competency, yet they have little or no control over their thoughts and actions. But there is little effort to test this meaningfully in our current system. This failure was confirmed as far back as 2006, when the U.S. Department of Justice's Bureau of Justice Statistics released a study showing that 64% of local jail inmates, 56% of state prisoners and 45% of federal prisoners had symptoms of serious mental illnesses. Prior to that study, it had been estimated that no more than about 20% of offenders had any mental health issues. And even these numbers aren't ironclad, as many mental illnesses remain undiagnosed.

The numbers are no more encouraging for death row inmates. The nebulous nature of mental illness has allowed states to continue executing borderline and mentally disturbed people at an alarming rate. In 2015, of the 28 people executed, approximately 75% were mentally impaired or disabled, experienced extreme childhood trauma and abuse, or were of questionable guilt. An examination of the 2015 cases that resulted in execution reveal a disturbing pattern: It's frequently not just one impairment, such as a low IQ score, that defines these cases, but rather multiple forms of disability and impairment.

And research has suggested that mentally ill defendants are more likely to give false confessions and are generally more vulnerable to coercion and intimidation to give false information. Additionally, they usually have difficulty comprehending their Miranda Rights, and frequently waive their right to counsel. Mentally ill defendants often lack the ability to even form criminal intent. Even when deemed competent to stand trial, and even where an insanity plea fails, mental illness can often prevent a defendant from forming the specific intent to commit the crimes for which they are charged, yet are still often found guilty. And this is even more prejudicial in capital cases, where such a finding may result in the execution of a mentally ill defendant.

Researchers in 2017 concluded that at least 43% of the inmates executed between 2000 and 2015 had received a mental illness diagnosis at some point in their lives. However, the researches cautioned that this number "probably underestimated the prevalence of mental illness - necessarily leaving out those who are undiagnosed, or for whom a diagnosis was not presented at trial or in the sources [...] reviewed." They also noted that trauma, while not a mental illness, is a risk factor for mental illness, and death row inmates are up to 4 times more likely to have suffered childhood trauma than the national average. It is also well-accepted that childhood trauma's long-term effects include higher likelihood of disrupted neurodevelopment, cognitive impairment, mental illness, and becoming the perpetrator or victim of violence.

Just in 2015, half of the inmates who were executed had an intellectual impairment, brain injury or serious mental illness. In addition to Warren Hill and Cecil Clay, discussed earlier, 12 others were executed with varying levels of mental disability, including Juan Garcia who had an IQ of 75 and was condemned to death at the age of 18.; Robert Charles who had a 67 IQ and was said to be "rather obviously retarded" by a psychiatrist employed by the state; Andrew Brennan who was a Vietnam veteran with post-traumatic stress disorder and bipolar disorder who was categorized as 100% disabled by the V.A.;

and Kent Spouse, who was diagnosed schizophrenic and who was "psychotic, paranoid, believed people were persecuting him, and did not understand the wrongfulness of his conduct" according to a court-appointed psychiatrist. Remarkably, none of these mental deficiencies met the threshold of proof, established by the various states.

One thing that should be clear from the data is that 1) a large percentage of criminal defendants are mentally impaired in some form or another; and 2) that our justice system has an insufficiently rigorous process for determining when a defendant is mentally disabled. Thus, many of the prisoners that we send to death row, and that are executed by the states, may have some mental or emotional disability that limits their exercise of free will, or their ability to understand the consequences of their actions, or the nature of the circumstances in which they find themselves. And while these are exactly the types of people that are supposed to be protected by the various standards herein discussed, they are far too often allowed to proceed, even when their handicaps are pointed out.

So, without calling for an outright ban on capital punishment in this country - I do, but just for the sake of argument - I would at least call for the United States to adopt a national standard for determining when a person should be exempt from the death penalty on the basis of mental illness or handicap. And that national standard should be based on scientific consensus and reason, without the subjective legal analyses so often implicit in our current system. In doing so, we may still claim to be a pro-capital punishment nation, while in practice the actual number of executions carried out will drop precipitously. That way we can still be one of the very few developed nations that allow capital punishment, but not one of the countries that executes the most people (occasionally even wrongfully-convicted people). It's a win-win situation - kind of.

XX.
To Plea Or Not to Plea

In the United States, every year tens of millions of people are charged with traffic offenses, misdemeanors and/or felonies. Approximately 95% of those cases resolve either through guilty pleas or other pre-trial devices. In other words, only about 5% of criminal cases actually go to trial. So prevalent is the guilty plea - almost always by means of a plea bargain - that a rather large body of caselaw and precedent has developed around just this concept. As most things in the realm of criminal procedure, there are important Constitutional questions that arise during the plea bargain process, and thus the Supreme Court has influenced this area of law immensely.

Let's start with the most basic question - what is a plea bargain, or for that matter a guilty plea itself? When a person is charged with a crime, recall that it is the prosecuting authority, be it the District Attorney, Attorney General, or U.S. Attorney, that brings these charges. Charging people with crimes is an executive function, and is the sole province of the executive branch of government. In other words, Courts - the judicial branch - are limited in how they can influence the charging of crimes, at least prior to trial. At any time during the life of a case - up to the day of trial - a criminal defendant has the ability to plead guilty to the charges against him. The judge would then sentence the defendant in accordance with the statute that the defendant pled guilty under. While this does happen spontaneously on occasion - usually a first time offender with a relatively minor offense - guilty pleas are usually made pursuant to a plea bargain. A plea bargain is nothing more than an agreement by the prosecutor to offer a reduction of the charge, or an agreement to recommend a lighter sentence to the judge, in exchange for the defendant's plea of guilty. A guilty plea is the same as a conviction.

Of course there are many reasons why people accept plea bargains and plead guilty. Most often, they are offered a substantial reduction in penalty. For example, in a hypothetical case, a defendant is charged with Possession with Intent to Distribute Cocaine, a second class felony. If found guilty at trial, the sentencing range, written into the statute itself, is 2 years to 30 years at hard labor. That means that if the defendant went to trial and lost, the judge could sentence him up to the maximum of 30 years in prison. If the district attorney wanted to resolve the case for whatever reason, he may offer to reduce the charge to a Simple Possession, which would only carry a maximum of 5 years and no minimum. Thus, if the defendant would accept that plea bargain, as a first time offender, he would probably be placed on probation, instead of having to serve time in prison. It is this choice - the choice between possible prison time and probation that encourages many first time offenders to plead guilty *in lieu* of trial - even if the State's case is less than airtight.

A more complicated scenario would be someone who has prior felony convictions. Because of prior convictions, a defendant would be referred to as a habitual offender, and would be facing increased penalties as a result. Under federal law and most state's laws, habitual offender statutes have been enacted to severely punish recidivists. In Louisiana, for example, if you have one previous felony conviction and you are convicted of a second one, the sentencing range under the habitual offender statute requires that the defendant be sentenced to a minimum 50% of the maximum penalty prescribed by law, up to a maximum of double the statutory maximum. In other words, if Bam Bam was a second felony offender charged with the same crime as Sammie, he would be facing a minimum of 15 years (1/2 of the maximum of 30 years) up to a maximum of 60 years (2 times the maximum). Plea bargains for multiple offenders therefore usually entail an agreement by the prosecutor to refrain from filing a habitual offender action. They might say if Bam Bam agrees to plead guilty as charged and serves at least 5 years in prison, they wouldn't charge him as a second offender, where the minimum would be at least 15 years in prison.

So, we know what a plea bargain is, and why people choose to accept them, now let's talk about the procedural framework. The first bedrock principle in determining whether a guilty plea is constitutional is the idea that the plea must be a knowing, intelligent, free and voluntary act on the part of the defendant. He must be afforded a right to counsel during the plea bargaining process and must make an intelligent waiver of his rights to proceed to trial and confront and cross examine his accusers. The Supreme Court codified this procedure in the case of <u>Boykin v. Alabama</u>. The <u>Boykin</u> court noted:

"A plea of guilty is more than a confession which admits that the accused did various acts; it is itself a conviction; nothing remains but to give judgment and determine punishment.[1] Admissibility of a confession must be based on a 'reliable determination on the voluntariness issue which satisfies the constitutional rights of the defendant.'" [2]

The Court went on to state that several federal constitutional rights are involved in a waiver that takes place when a plea of guilty is entered in a criminal trial. First, is the privilege against compulsory self-incrimination guaranteed by the Fifth Amendment and applicable to the States by reason of the Fourteenth, pursuant to <u>Malloy v. Hogan</u>, 378 U.S. 1. Second, is the right to trial by jury, pursuant to <u>Duncan v. Louisiana</u>, 391 U.S. 145. Third, is the right to confront one's accusers, pursuant to <u>Pointer v. Texas</u>, 380 U.S. 400. "We cannot presume a waiver of these three important federal rights from a silent record."

In other words, the <u>Boykin</u> Court set forth a requirement in criminal cases that a record be made of the defendant's voluntary waiver of these rights in open court. Courts have thus adopted written forms that are presented to the defendant which lists all the rights the defendant is waiving by entering a plea of guilty. The defendant signs this form after reviewing it, preferably with an attorney, and then it is read out loud by the Judge on the official court record, and the defendant is required to answer out loud that he is making a free and voluntary waiver of his constitutional rights. This has become known as a "Boykin" hearing, and the form is generally referred to as a "Boykin" form.

As it concerns plea bargains, while there is no absolute right to a plea bargain, the Supreme Court has made it clear that if a plea bargain is offered, then the prosecutor making the offer must keep any promises made. The Supreme Court decision in

<u>Santobello v. New York</u> is the leading case in this matter. There, the court indicated that there must be fairness in securing an agreement between an accused and a prosecutor. Additionally, as the court noted:

The accused pleading guilty must be counseled, absent a waiver. [T[he sentencing judge must develop, on the record, the factual basis for the plea, as, for example, by having the accused describe the conduct that gave rise to the charge. The plea must, of course, be voluntary and knowing and if it was induced by promises, the essence of those promises must in some way be made known.

The Court did state that there is no absolute right to have a guilty plea *accepted.* [3] In other words, even if a defendant is offered a plea bargain, a Judge may reject a plea in the "exercise of sound judicial discretion."

The Court in <u>Blackledge v. Allison</u> famously stated: "[W]hatever might be the situation in an ideal world, the fact is that the guilty plea and the often concomitant plea bargain are important components of this country's criminal justice system. Properly administered, they can benefit all concerned." [4] However, regardless of how important plea bargaining may be in the administration of criminal justice, we are reminded that "a guilty plea is a serious and sobering occasion inasmuch as it constitutes a waiver of the fundamental rights to a jury trial, to confront one's accusers, to present witnesses in one's defense, to remain silent, and to be convicted by proof beyond all reasonable doubt."

Since <u>Kercheval v. United States,</u> 274 U.S. 220, the courts have recognized "that 'unfairly obtained' guilty pleas . . . ought to be vacated." In other words, if a defendant does not knowingly waive his rights, or if he has been misled, or the record indicates that he wasn't fully apprised of his rights or the consequences of his plea, the defendant can withdraw his guilty plea. But as long as the prosecutor doesn't blatantly deceive the defendant or break promises following a plea bargain, and the court conducts an adequate Boykin hearing, it is generally very difficult for a defendant to change his mind after he pleads guilty.

Reasons supporting the withdrawal of a guilty plea would ordinarily include breach of a plea bargain, inducement, misleading advice of counsel, strength of the evidence of actual guilt or the like. A mere change of heart or mind by the defendant as to whether he made a good bargain will not ordinarily support allowing the withdrawal of a bargained guilty plea. Without fraud, intimidation or incompetence of counsel, a guilty plea is not made less voluntary or informed by the considered advice of counsel. Misunderstandings between the defendant and his defense counsel do not render a guilty plea involuntary.[5] In other words, unless you can show some pretty unusual circumstances, if you plead guilty, you are stuck with that guilty plea.

And as I've already stated, guilty pleas and plea bargains are absolutely indispensable in the efficient administration of justice. Without them, we would be forced to go to trial in every single case, which would place an insurmountable burden on the court system. There simply aren't enough courts, judges, attorneys or hours in the day for every criminal case to go to a full trial on the merits. The system is already overworked and buckling under its own weight, and that's with only 5% of the cases going to trial. Increasing that burden

20 fold would bring the whole thing to a screeching halt, which would, in turn, result in many cases being thrown out on Speedy Trial grounds. This is one of the primary reasons that prosecutors even offer plea bargains in the first place. Another reason plea bargains are offered is when the prosecution perceives a weakness in their case. In order to get a conviction, they will cut a deal so the offender doesn't get off "scot free". And perhaps - hopefully - sometimes the idea behind offering plea bargains is the age-old battle between harsh justice and mercy. We want criminals to pay a price, but we also need compassion and forgiveness and understand that people occasionally step out of line, and we shouldn't over-punish if we want to maintain a civil society.

On the other hand, all those important considerations aside, there is no doubt that plea bargains are overused, and often maliciously so. Defendants are lured into pleading guilty on cases that they might have a good chance of winning at trial. Innocent people take plea bargains to avoid the threat of long prison sentences. We actually even have a judicial acknowledgment of this scenario, pursuant to the case of North Carolina v. Alford, which stands for the proposition that a defendant can choose to plead guilty without confessing guilt if he feels a plea would be in his "best interests." In other words, courts know that sometimes defendants are innocent - or at least believe they are innocent - yet still plead guilty because of the threat of a long prison sentence. Recall that the State holds pretty much all the cards in criminal cases. And young men, disproportionately African American, are loaded into the system, often unfairly, and often without knowing the full consequences of a felony

179

conviction. And again, this is why competent and thoughtful legal counsel is so necessary at all stages of criminal proceedings.

CHAPTER EIGHT
Toward Economic Equality

"We can have democracy in this country, or we can have great wealth concentrated in the hands of the few, but we cant have both."

\- Louis D. Brandeis

XXI.
Massive Wealth Inequality Threatens American Exceptionalism

The Oxfam report released in 2018 showed what anyone who's paying attention already knew - the wealth gap between the super rich and everyone else is getting wider. According to the latest report by the international charity confederation, Oxfam International, the richest 1% own 82% of the world's wealth. Just 42 billionaires have as much wealth as the poorest 50% of the population - approximately 3.6 billion people. Just think about those numbers. Somehow, even looking at those numbers, some of the smartest people I know refuse to believe that the deck is stacked, the game is rigged. And even though the top 1% has seen their wealth skyrocket at the same time the average earnings for workers remained stagnant, smart people still insist that our current system is fair. Even as we have seen class mobility drop to its lowest rate since before 1970, the delusion persists that people who aren't rich just don't work as hard as those 42 people.

Just focusing on the American economy, there is now an alarming disparity between the richest Americans, and everybody else, and that disparity is affecting the economic prosperity of our nation, and threatens a bleak outlook for the future. Prior to about 1980, the wealth gap was much more ideal. The 1950's and 1960's saw the birth of a robust middle class that was one of the strongest in history. While infrastructure expansion and a strong post-World War II economy certainly contributed to our mutual prosperity, there was also heavy support for unions and progressive taxation, along with vigorous anti-trust policies that ensured that the rich did not dominate and subvert the less wealthy.

The current extreme trend of wealth inequality is rather neatly traced back to the Reagan years. Ronald Reagan was a fierce opponent of unions and collective bargaining. Under his command, anti-trust laws were eased, financial markets were deregulated, and tax rates were slashed to historic lows. Reagan coined the phrase "trickle-down" economics, suggesting that as the rich got richer, their excessive wealth would trickle down to the masses. Of course, this has proven to be a complete myth.

While economic gains were made under Bill Clinton, he did little to stem the growing wealth gap. Deregulation continued under Clinton, and while many sectors of society saw modest upward mobility, most of the wealth generated during his tenure went to the richest Americans. And any gains that **were** made under Clinton were almost immediately reversed under George W. Bush. There was an almost immediate reversion to the "trickle down" economic ideas of Reagan that has since set the U.S. on a downward spiral of economic depression. Well, at least for most of us. You see, the richest Americans have gotten obscenely richer, while most Americans have seen a sharp decline in virtually every metric of success and financial well-being, a trend that unfortunately continued under Barrack Obama, and has become even more stark under Trump and his cabinet of billionaires. In fact, Trump's sole achievement in his first year is a tax bill designed to funnel over a trillion dollars to the mega-wealthy.

Ratings agency Standard & Poor's issued a report in 2014 stating that the actual income gap in the U.S. has been worsening and now is approaching an "extreme" threshold that threatens to hamper long-term economic growth. According to experts (and logic), the wealth gap undermines economic growth by dampening social mobility and creating a less-educated workforce unable to compete in the global economy. "Higher levels of income inequality increase political pressures, discouraging trade, investment, and hiring," the report noted.

Inequality serves as a "wedge" between growth and living standards, funneling income to the most wealthy, and making it more difficult for living standards to improve, or for poverty to fall, during business expansions. Economic growth, therefore, "has become a spectator sport for too many poor and middle-class households." In fact, following the most recent recession, the stock market has rebounded to its highest level in history, GDP is up significantly, corporate profits and worker productivity are at historical highs, yet median household income is actually down 5%. So the rich have seen massive income growth, while everyone else is seeing their incomes fall or stagnate.

Ultimately, a lopsided economy that benefits a smaller and smaller portion of the populace, can, and does, lead to economic collapse. Many economists now agree that both the Great Depression and the most-recent recession in 2008, were caused - at least in part - by extreme levels of wealth and income inequality. The greed and unfairness that such a

185

system encourages leads to eroding levels of opportunity and mobility for all income levels, and will eventually lead to disaster if we don't take action to preserve the fundamental American principal of equal opportunity. And despite the 2008 collapse, and a resulting "economic recovery," inequality has continued to grow.

There is a video on YouTube called "Wealth Inequality in America." This video was created a few years ago, and has since gone viral with almost 20 million views. It shows three different wealth distribution charts, one showing what most Americans believe is the "Ideal" wealth distribution, one showing what most Americans believe is the actual distribution, and then, a chart showing what the actual distribution really is. Of course, the difference is shocking, at least to average Americans.

Basically, taking data from a Harvard poll conducted a few years ago, the first chart shows the "ideal" wealth distribution as reported by a majority of those polled. It shows a very healthy income curve, starting with the bottom 20% almost completely above the poverty line, with a smooth transition between all levels, and a top 20% that is only about 10-20 times wealthier than the poorest folks.

Of course, most Americans know that our wealth distribution is anything but "ideal," thus, when they described what they believed the distribution actually is, the response showed a graph that was much more skewed toward the wealthy. This graph shows the bottom 20% quite a bit worse off, with a small portion actually below the poverty line, and it shows the wealthiest Americans with roughly 100 times the wealth of the poorest, and even a middle class that is struggling a bit.

The shocking thing is that this graph is nowhere near the actual distribution of wealth. In the actual distribution graph, the poorest don't even register, and almost the entire lowest 20% is below the poverty line, while the middle class is barely distinguishable from the poor. And of course, the top 1% is so far off the chart that there had to be a special column just for his portion of the wealth - roughly 40% of the overall wealth of the nation, concentrated in the hands of 1% of the people.

In the U.S, the wealth gap has reached "spectacular" heights. And the rich are actually wealthier than previously thought. It is estimated that America's top 1 percent, the nation's wealthiest group by a long shot, control almost 40 percent of wealth, rather than the 30 percent that had previously been estimated. Let that sink in. The top 1% has nearly half of the nation's wealth. While the bottom 50% only has 7% of the wealth. The 1% has more than five times as much wealth as the entire lower half of this nation's population.

The richest 1% earn almost 25% of the nation's annual income, while in 1976 they only took home about 9%. 82% of the total value of stocks and investments is owned by the top 10%, while 54% of Americans have zero. Obviously, the bottom 50% of the country is not investing, just barely earning enough to get by. CEOs of our richest corporations take home somewhere around 380 times as much income as the same rich corporation's average worker - not its lowest paid employees, but the average earner. That means the average worker would need to work an entire month to earn what the CEO makes in a single hour of a single day. And again, this is a trend that we have seen grow steadily more pronounced since the 1970's, and the end of the economic policies of the 40's, 50's and 60's that helped create the most robust middle class in world history.

This picture of the American economy strongly suggests an uneven playing field. As the rich get richer, the poor get poorer, until virtually all of the nation's wealth is controlled - either directly or indirectly - by a handful of mega-wealthy individuals. When enough wealth is concentrated in the hands of a few billionaires, it becomes easier for those few billionaires to buy politicians, to repeal regulations, skew the tax code in their favor, thus allowing them to keep even more of their wealth, and to pay their workers less and less, while eliminating any competition.

In fact, the recent Oxfam report specifically cited "tax evasion, erosion of worker's rights, cost-cutting, and businesses' influence on policy decisions" as reasons for the widening inequality. Mark Godlring, and Oxfam executive, said the numbers indicate "something is very wrong with the global economy... the concentration of extreme wealth at the top is not a sign of a thriving economy but a symptom of a system that is failing the millions of hard-working people on poverty wages who make our clothes and grow our food."

"Oh, you're just jealous. Don't attack rich people because they worked for what they got." I know, i know, anytime anyone starts talking about income and wealth inequality, some libertarian zealot hollers "Class Warfare." There is a vocal group of opponents that view every mention of inequality as a challenge to the rich and powerful. A battle cry by the

188

poor masses against the wealthy elite that are literally in charge of everything. They are the "job creators" and we should all be thankful for their contributions to our society - and the crumbs they throw to working class Americans. But these wealthy titans are busy buying elections, and influencing public policy, and consolidating economic power by engaging in unhindered mega-mergers, all to make it even harder for hard-working people to achieve that mythical American Dream. And don't forget that the majority of the nation's wealthiest didn't exactly "work for what they got."   Almost 2/3 of those on the Forbes 400 list were *born* rich, and will do anything to preserve that legacy for their progeny. As Warren Buffet - a mega-wealthy proponent of capitalism himself - once stated, "There's class warfare alright, but it's *my* class, the rich class, that's making war." And we, the intrepid 99%, are the casualties of that war. Think about that.

XXII.
Free College is Freedom of Opportunity and Benefits Society At-Large

IT is no protected secret that I have been a dedicated supporter of Democratic Socialist, Bernie Sanders, in his bid for the Democratic presidential nomination. I am a full-on, dyed-in-the-wool, bleeding-heart progressive, and I am very proud of it. I support Sanders – and the revolution that he helped launch - not because he is attractive, well-mannered, honest and genuine, but because his beliefs and policy proposals are firmly rooted in progressive liberal values. Healthcare for all, Civil Rights, LGBT rights, mandatory living wages, and tuition-free public universities - I believe in all these things, as Senator Sanders does, not because I like "free stuff" but because all of these things will most certainly lead to a better society for all Americans. And I am actually shocked that the proposal that seems to get the most inordinate amount of attention and criticism is free college tuition.

Since at least the middle of the 1800's, the United States has attempted to provide a primary school education to most of its children. By 1870, every state in the country had free public schools, and not coincidentally the U.S. had the highest literacy rate in the world. In the following decades, forward-thinking educators began to call for the adoption of "post-literacy" education for the masses, which, they argued, would "improve citizenship, develop higher-order traits, and produce the managerial and professional leadership needed for rapid economic modernization." And again, the U.S. was alone in this endeavor, being the first industrialized nation to promote secondary education, i.e. high school, for a majority of Americans. While around the turn of the century, the percentage of citizens with a high school diploma was less than 10%, by 1940 that number had risen to over 50%, again making the U.S. unique in the world. And of course, the number of high school graduates continued to rise as it became clear that a high school education was necessary to keep up with a technologically advancing society.

In the intervening years between the "Baby Boomers" and the current generation, the same classical high school education became ever more important, but also ever less sufficient to meet the demands of an increasingly automated society. Our forebears had to become educated, at least through high school, in order to compete in an industrial age. However beginning around the 1960's, the industrial age succumbed to the 'Information Age," a time of advanced technology, computerized everything, a global economy - and the challenges are greater than at any time in history. Now, that high school education that got you so far in 1940 can only get you half as far - if that. In the new technological era, and what lies beyond, a college degree is the minimum educational level necessary to remain competitive.

And we have seen a steady increase in college enrollment and graduation rates for many years. About 63% of high school graduates now enroll in college, the highest enrollment percentage ever, and over 1/3 of them earn a degree. And the trend continues to rise into the future. However, while college is becoming more and more necessary, the costs have continued to rise, and fewer and fewer people can afford it. This has led to a high dropout rate, massive and oppressive student loan debt, and an outright barrier to entry for many people. But we have the resources to alleviate this problem, and we must, or we will be left behind. Many other countries already offer free public college, and the U.S. is already lagging in educational attainment. In 1995, the U.S. was number 1, however in 2012 we were 19th (out of the top 28 OECD member nations).

Public universities should be tuition-free, just like primary and secondary schools. We have always adjusted our educational aspirations to fit the complexities of the day, and it is time to do it again. A more educated population will have immediate, and broadly-based benefits to society as a whole, including increased innovation and economic growth. But more importantly, the current and next generations will be better prepared to address the challenges of the future, and to compete in an ever-more-complex global "mediaverse."

Most people seem to understand the growing need for a college-educated populace. Most people agree that going to college should be affordable, and that student loan debt is overly oppressive. However, those same people refuse to believe that we should finance such a system. "I can't pay for my own college, how am I going to pay for someone else?!" I hear this often. And I agree, adding another huge expenditure to our already-bloated federal budget would just be more burdensome on us lowly taxpayers. But upon closer inspection, it's not as bad as most people might think.

In a recent study by the Department of Education, it was determined that public universities collected approximately $62 billion of tuition in a year. That may sound like a lot of money (it is), but consider that we spend more than ten (10) times that much on our military ($800 billion), the highest military budget in the world.

In fact, we spend more on our military than the next 14 highest-spending nations *combined*. If we cut our military budget in half, we would still outspend our closest rival, China, by almost $100 billion! So we could afford to tighten that belt just a little, don't you think? Well, you may not even have to. You see, we also already have a relatively high expenditure for higher education programs, like grants, tax benefits, and other financial aid - about $69 billion.

That's right, $69 billion - $7 billion **more** than $62 billion. And a lot of that is going to private, for-profit institutions. So you see, Dorothy, you actually already *are* paying for someone else to go to college - at an overpriced *private* university, instead of a perfectly suitable public one.

By scaling back the financial aid programs that we currently offer in order to make college attainable and affordable to some students, we could make college attainable for ALL students. And it would have the added benefit of eliminating a large percentage of the student loan debt that is currently burdening college graduates and stifling the economy. Many recent graduates are unable to buy a home, save money, or invest. In fact, an inordinate number of college graduates still receive substantial support from their families, and they are having a difficult time surviving at all. These are definitely not conditions conducive to innovation and entrepreneurship, and we should certainly not foment such conditions. The only logical thing to do to ensure America's continued relevance in the global economy is to change the way we finance higher education.

This plan works. In countries around the world, including France, Scotland, Germany, and numerous others, public universities are tuition free. It can work here, by simply re-allocating current expenditures away from private schools and into public schools. And I don't need to point out that some of the best schools in the world are American public universities, including Georgia Tech, UCLA and USC, among others. A guaranteed education at any of our public universities would help make America the envy of the world once again. While we continue to exult in our own "exceptionalism," we are falling behind in virtually every metric of well-being - in health, we are 31st place, 69th in ecosystem sustainability, 39th in basic education, 34th in access to water and sanitation and 31st in personal safety.

I know it's a lot to think about. To think that your tax dollars may be going to provide an education for some poor kid halfway across the country while you weren't able to afford to send your own kids to college may be a hard pill to swallow. However, even here in America, public universities used to be free - that's what "Public" used to mean. The public university system was established so that any American citizen who wanted to attain a higher education, could. It has only happened in the past couple decades that greed, corruption and corporate influence has turned America's top-rated education system into the money machine that it is today. And it is unfortunate if you were one of the unlucky ones that got screwed by that corrupted system. But if America wants to regain its position of prestige, and we want to ensure that our kids and grandkids enjoy a brighter and better tomorrow, we have to start today. And with minimal effort, and practically zero extra expense, we can do it. I won't say that free college is **the** moral dilemma of the day, but it is definitely one of them. And with a more educated populace, we will be better equipped to deal with the other ones.

CHAPTER NINE
Celebrating Death

"Facts are stubborn things; and whatever may be our wishes, our inclinations, or the dictates of our passions, they cannot alter the state of facts and evidence."

- John Adams

XXIII.
Nancy Reagan and the Whitewashing of Memory to Honor the Dead

In 2015, Americans bid farewell to former First Lady, Nancy Reagan, who passed away at the age of 94. After her marriage to Ronald Reagan in 1951, she left behind her own career in Hollywood to stand by and support her husband through his political career, both as Governor of California and then as President of the United States. It is hard to muster any animus toward the beloved Nancy Reagan, as she remains one of the most influential and fondly-remembered presidential spouses in modern history. And I will not even attempt to tarnish her reputation as a loving, patriotic, and concerned public figure for most of the last half-century. She tried to make the world a little nicer, a little more compassionate, and a little more human. And she gave us her son, the inimitable Ron Reagan, who is a national treasure and remains active in politics and public awareness today..

But, despite the predilection of most media pundits, politicians and celebrities to lionize a public figure out of respect, I feel it is a grave error to embellish someone's record just because they die – it robs us, and our progeny, of the benefit of honest reflection. So, despite my benevolence, I believe that it's important to remember exactly what people like Nancy Reagan did during their lives, whether or not it is flattering.

What Nancy Reagan was perhaps most widely

associated with was her trademark campaign to reduce drug use among young people. In the 1980's, while Ronald was president, he declared that drug abuse was a threat to our national security, and doubled down on the War on Drugs originally begun under Nixon a decade earlier. Nancy, in what I only hope was based on compassion and sincerity, turned her focus to school programs such as D.A.R.E., in an effort to reduce teen drug abuse. She coined the famous catchphrase on national television, which became a ubiquitous slogan throughout the 80's - "Just Say No!"

Throughout her time as First Lady, Nancy appeared in commercial after commercial and Public Service Announcement after Public Service Announcement, to warn Americans of the harms and evils of illicit drug use. She urged children to resist peer pressure to experiment with drugs, and she urged parents, teachers, school administrators, and the public to report any illegal drug activity without exception. The results of her tireless campaign are disputed. There is no evidence that any of it did any good. But, I guess, she meant well. Unfortunately, perhaps naively unintentional, she was part of a larger problem, greatly intensified by her husband, that has swelled the prison-industrial complex, and has destroyed countless more lives than drug abuse ever could on its own.

First of all, the idea that teaching "abstinence only," and asking kids to resist peer pressure, will have some great deterrent effect on drug use is illogical, and not backed by any empirical research. In fact, high school students who enrolled in programs like D.A.R.E. ("Drug Abuse Resistance Education") and other abstinence only programs, were statistically just as likely to experiment with drugs as any other group.

199

Critics of these programs advocate harm-reduction education to be taught alongside these use-reduction strategies. This approach recognizes the fact that some teens are going to use drugs and they should be educated on risk-reduction and safe practices.

Besides attempting to reduce the drug abuse problem to a single slogan, programs such as Just Say No fail because they fail to recognize what leads to drug abuse in the first place. Just Say No, and the larger War on Drugs and Tough On Crime movements of the 80's and 90's, sought to marginalize drug users, excluding them from society, and labeling drug use and addiction as "evil," and dangerous to society. They used high profile cases of teens who died from overdose deaths, or other horrific incidents involving illegal narcotics, to show people how "bad" drugs are, and that the only answer is to eradicate drugs and to remove drug users and dealers from society through the use of "zero-tolerance" approaches to enforcement. The Reagans helped make it popular in America, and to a lesser extent around the world, to address drug abuse as a purely Criminal problem, instead of as a Public Health problem.

That approach to drug abuse has had dire consequences on America, particularly in the minority communities. Laws have been enacted to provide unconscionably harsh penalties on drug dealers and users alike. Law enforcement has been given incentives to aggressively pursue drug crimes, which has led to the over-militarization of the police, severe erosion of civil liberties, and the marginalization of poor and working-class families. The War on Drugs has caused America's prison population to explode, from less than 200,000 in the 1970's to more than 2 million today - more than any other country on Earth, both as a percentage of population and as an absolute number.   And a shocking percentage of these prisoners are incarcerated for minor drug possession charges.

When people are arrested, charged and convicted of drug crimes, they not only go to prison (with abusive mandatory sentencing guidelines), but their families suffer. That person is no longer able to provide for his family during his incarceration, often leaving children behind to be cared for by a single parent, who often has to work two jobs to scrape by. And when he does get released from prison, he has a felony record which makes it difficult for him to find a decent job, disqualifies him for public assistance, including financial aid, and makes it extremely difficult to rise out of poverty. And we wonder why these same people end up back on the streets doing the same thing that got them there in the first place. Recidivism is, in many instances, a self-fulfilling prophesy. It is absolutely immoral to deprive a human being of his freedom, and to subject him and his family to a lifetime of hardship and poverty, over a poor decision to ingest an intoxicating substance.

Just Say No, and other such programs, approach the complex issues inherent in drug abuse and addiction with the false premise that "peer pressure" is the driving force - monkey see monkey do. In reality, people take recreational drugs for a variety of reasons, including desperation, unhappiness, depression, and various socio-economic factors. Drugs promise an escape, if only temporary, from the miseries of life. But addressing those problems is complicated - it involves society-wide reforms, with education, job creation and training, and mental health services for the poor and middle class, all things that the Reagan administration, and its neoconservative ideology that has been adopted by most of today's Republicans, worked against. Instead, it is easier, and indeed it is another hallmark of the Reagan legacy, to blame individual choices on all of society's ills. If you're poor and struggling you must be a lazy leech, and if you choose to take drugs, you must be a weak-minded criminal. Arresting and locking up the weak-minded criminals is easier than fixing the underlying problems that lead to illicit drug use, and it makes us look like we are doing something by fighting the scourge of narcotics with "Tough Love."

I could cite statistics showing how devastating the War on Drugs has been - from the 1.5 million Americans that are arrested every year, to the 1 trillion (that's a 1 followed by 12 zeros) dollars of taxpayer money that has been used to wage this pointless war, and thousands of innocent people who's lives have been irreversibly damaged - but I will save that for another article. The bottom line is that people don't do drugs because their friend tells them to, any more than a person refrains from doing drugs because of the criminal consequences. Believe me, drugs are just as easy to get today as they were 40 years ago, despite decades of more and more oppressive punishment for drug-related crimes. Drugs are a problem that can, and should, be addressed with common sense public health initiatives. Rehabilitation programs, job training, mental health services, and other community based efforts to improve the lives and prospects of at-risk citizens would not only be orders of magnitude less expensive than the failed Drug War, but will have

more effective, and more humane, outcomes. So to
you, Nancy Reagan, I say thank you for your years of
tireless public service and your undoubtedly noble
efforts, but we must Just Say No to programs and
initiatives that seek to reduce our nation's host of
complicated socio-economic problems, to easy-to-
digest but largely ineffectual ad campaigns that exist
only to make our ruling class feel like they are
compassionate - and superior. "Just Say No" - like me
- it's easy. Yeah, it's easy, if you have the life of Nancy
Reagan.

XXIV.
Justice Antonin Scalia and the Politics of Death

2016 saw the passing of Justice Antonin Scalia, who was a member of the United States Supreme Court since his appointment by Ronald Reagan in 1986. Scalia was a very strong-willed and stubborn jurist who adhered to an "originalist" view of the Constitution and its Amendments - meaning that he interpreted the Constitution to mean what it meant at the time of the original drafting - and he resisted any attempt to interpret it as a "living" document that changed with society. He was, at times, brash, vehement, and unapologetic, but he was at ALL times a legal scholar and prolific writer, composing more concurring opinions than any other Justice in history, and his volume of dissenting opinions was only exceeded by two other Justices. In other words, he had strong convictions, and he was determined to let everyone know what they were. As a lawyer, and self-proclaimed legal scholar, myself, I have great respect and reverence for the Justice, and I mourn his death. However, as a liberal, and self-proclaimed progressive humanist, my emotions are slightly more complicated.

Scalia was most certainly considered a "conservative" Justice. He was against abortion, making it extraordinarily clear that he wanted to overturn *Roe v. Wade*. He railed against the majority in *Webster v. Reproductive Health Services*, when the Court declined to overturn *Roe v. Wade*. Scalia was strongly opposed to affirmative action, voting against programs that provided quotas in awarding public contracts or allowing universities to consider race in admissions. He was opposed to gay marriage, as was readily apparent in his lengthy and scathing dissent in *Obergfell v. Hodges*. He was a gun rights activist, and defined the term "well-regulated militia" as it appears in the text of the Second Amendment as meaning "the body of all citizens." And of course, he was a strong supporter of capital punishment. Not only did he believe capital punishment to be Constitutional, but he was hesitant to place ANY restrictions on its use. He advocated for the death penalty to be applied to minors (people who committed a capital offense while still under the age of 17), and even to mentally handicapped people, arguing that the authors of the Constitution would not have had a problem executing a person that was "mildly mentally retarded."

His extremely conservative bias notwithstanding, Scalia also joined more liberal views on several criminal law issues. For instance, he authored the opinion in *Kyllo v. United States*, where the majority found that thermal imaging of a person's home without a search warrant was a violation of the Fourth Amendment's prohibition against unlawful searches and seizures, thereby overturning the defendant's conviction for growing marijuana in his home. He also voted against a statute that allowed a sentencing judge to enhance a criminal defendant's sentence if the judge found that the underlying crime was a "hate crime", stating that the Sixth Amendment requires that the prosecution prove to a jury every element of a crime, including whether or not it was a hate crime. He likewise ruled in favor of criminal defendants in several cases concerning a defendant's absolute right to confront his accusers, including victims of child abuse, and lab technicians in drug cases.

Regardless of my own opinions of Antonin Scalia, he will certainly be remembered as an intellectual and an activist judge. He voted his conscience, and was very adamant about his views. Unfortunately, he also let his views on religion cloud his impartiality too often. Many of his decisions relating to homosexuality and same-sex marriage were undoubtedly motivated by his strong Catholic faith. He believed that the devil walked amongst us, and he supported the idea that religious freedom should allow people to discriminate against certain groups, especially gay ones. Needless to say, many of his dogmatic and conservative views earned him great respect from conservative lawmakers, while earning him contempt from more liberal-minded politicians.

Justice Scalia's untimely death has left a void on the Supreme Court. Unfortunately for conservatives, especially those in Congress, it also leaves open the unfathomable opportunity for President Obama to appoint a replacement. Thus far in his 7 years in the Oval Office, Obama has had the privilege of appointing two (2) other justices - Sonia Sotomayor (who replaced Justice Souter) and Elena Kegan (who replaced Justice Stevens). However this vacancy is sure to be the most controversial, because where Sotomayer and Kegan both replaced liberal-leaning justices and therefore did not affect the balance of the High Court, the impending appointment will most certainly affect that balance. In the absence of Justice Scalia, the Court is comprised of four (4) conservative-leaning justices - John Roberts, Clarence Thomas, Anthony Kennedy, and Samuel Alito; and four liberal-leaning justices - Ruth Bader Ginsburg, Stephen Breyer, Sonia Sotomayor and Elena Kagan. Most controversial decisions in recent years have been split 5-4 based on these ideological lines, and the impeding appointment will have the potential to reverse some of the more unpopular ones.

For instance, in *Citizens United v. Federal Election Commission*, the majority essentially held that corporations have the right, under the First Amendment, to expend any amount of money advocating for issues (or for or against candidates) at any time. In doing so, the Court allowed rich and powerful corporations to exercise enormous control over the democratic process, claiming that corporations have the First Amendment right to freedom of speech, which includes their right to support or oppose candidates for public office. While traditionally the legal definition of corporations considered them to be "juridical persons," granting Constitutional rights to them is something our founding fathers would likely have chuckled over. And this decision has been derided and fiercely criticized for giving the rich disproportionate power over politics.

Likewise, the decision in *Burwell v. Hobby Lobby* was also decided by a 5-4 vote. Hobby Lobby complained that, under the Affordable Care Act ("Obamacare") companies that provided health insurance to its employees had to provide for certain types of contraception, including birth control pills. Hobby Lobby's management stated that contraception was against its religion and it should be protected from any mandate that requires it to ignore its religious convictions. The majority found that the ACA did violate Hobby Lobby's religious rights, and thus exempted Hobby Lobby, and others similarly situated, from the contraception mandate. This time, the Court essentially found that corporations also have religious freedom. Of course, more liberal minds found this decision to be appalling, and was essentially another way to allow corporations to discriminate against a certain class of people - women in this case.

Of course, we cannot predict whether the Supreme Court would take advantage of a new liberal-leaning majority (assuming Obama appoints a liberal-leaning justice to fill Scalia's vacancy), but the specter of such a perceived catastrophe is enough to rouse the conservatives into action. Thus, immediately upon his death, congressional Republicans, led by right-wing extremist and presidential hopeful, Ted Cruz, began calling for Congress to prevent Obama from nominating Scalia's replacement. Republicans claim that the next president should fill the vacancy because the "American people should have a voice in the selection of their next Supreme Court justice." And make no mistake, Congress will undoubtedly block any attempt by Obama to make that appointment.

While Ted Cruz praised Justice Scalia for his literal interpretation of the Constitution and his principled approach to upholding Constitutional values, he seems quite willing to ignore the very express provision of the Constitution that mandates - requires - the President and the Senate to fill Supreme Court vacancies. Clause 2, Article II of the Constitution expressly states that the President "...*shall* nominate, and by and with the Advice and Consent of the Senate, *shall* appoint ... Judges of the Supreme Court." It is not up for debate what this clause means.

It is the DUTY of the President and the DUTY of the Senate to appoint Judges of the Supreme Court. It doesn't say, "the Next President shall nominate," it says THE President. And, although Republicans refuse to acknowledge his legitimacy, Barrack Obama is currently the *only* President of the United States.

If we are to assume that there is any legal basis for the Republicans' proposition that we should wait until after the new president takes office in approximately 340 days, at what point do we cut that off? Only in the last year of a President's term? Or maybe with only 18 months left in office any president should be prohibited from making new appointments? What about half-way through his term? You see how quickly this argument could turn into something ridiculous. There is simply no legal basis to withhold appointment to fill Scalia's vacancy, yet Congressional Republicans, who often consider themselves "Constitutional Scholars," will be hellbent to thwart any effort by Obama to fulfill his Constitutional duty, thereby abdicating their own Constitutional duty at the same time. And why? Is it because they really think that selection of the Supreme Court justices should reflect the will of the voters? Or is it because they are determined to obstruct Barrack Obama in the hopes that their own candidate (whoever that might be) will win the general election and the balance of power in the Supreme Court will remain on their side? I'll let you decide the answer to that question.

In the wake of the Justice's death, the Supreme Court had 8 members, divided evenly between conservative and liberal voting records. Any divisive issue before the Court was therefore likely to be decided by a tied vote. A tied vote in the Supreme

Court is the same as no decision at all, and will result in the holding of the lower court remaining. In other words, waiting until the next president takes office to select Scalia's successor means, essentially, adjourning the U.S. Supreme Court for almost an entire year. We haven't even selected candidates for the next presidential election yet. It is unprecedented for a Supreme Court vacancy to remain for an entire year. But in a presidency that has been marked by aggressive obstructionism, government shutdowns, and blatant disrespect for the president himself, it is not surprising that the right-wing establishment would object to any attempt to replace Antonin Scalia with anyone other than Antonin Scalia. However, given Scalia's history of strict interpretation of the Constitution, it is reasonable to assume that even he would have objected to the Senate's refusal to perform its Article II duty to confirm a replacement in the ample span of eleven months. Thus, while Ted Cruz believes that "[w]e owe it to [Scalia] . . . for the Senate to ensure that the next President names his replacement," encouraging the Congress to abandon its Constitutional duty to select a replacement within the next calendar year would, indeed, *dis*honor Justice Scalia's legacy. Or, at least that's my opinion.

CHAPTER TEN
The War on Climate

"Climate Change is happening, humans are causing it, and I think this is perhaps the most serious environmental issue facing us."

- Bill Nye

XXV.
Climate Change Denial Is Real, And It Is A Serious Threat To Our Continued Existence

Believe it or not, there is overwhelming evidence that climate change is occurring on our planet, and that it is caused - at least in part - by human activity.   So-called "anthropogenic" climate change arises primarily through the use of fossil fuels, which release carbon dioxide (CO_2) into the atmosphere when they are burned. Cars, airplanes, power stations, and factories all burn fossil fuels that are filling our atmosphere with excess CO_2, which is in turn heating the atmosphere, and impacting our global climate. On November 23, 2018, a major report was issued by 13 federal agencies assessing the impact of climate change on the United States over the next several decades. The report concludes that if drastic action is not taken to halt global warming, the U.S. could suffer from disruption of supply chains, lower agricultural yields and increased damage by fire, as we've seen recently in California, and opening up the potential for the Southeast to experience similarly devastating forest fires.   In other words, we will see very visible consequences in just a few decades if climate change is not swiftly and decisively addressed.

Admittedly, it is the greenhouse effect that has allowed humans to evolve and thrive on Earth. Without sufficient levels of greenhouse gases in the atmosphere, atmospheric heat would be allowed to escape into outer space and be lost to the universe. So a certain level of these gases is beneficial, and indeed necessary to life on Earth.

However, there is such as thing as too much of a good thing. We need only look to our closest celestial neighbor, Venus, for an example of too much. Venus has been called Earth's twin. It is almost exactly the same size, mass, and volume. It has almost the exact same gravity, and it still lies inside the 'habitable zone' of the Sun, and it has a very dense atmosphere. But, the atmosphere of Venus is approximately 95% CO_2. The atmosphere is so heavy that the pressure at the surface is 92 times that of Earth's atmospheric pressure. And the temperature on the surface is about 900 degrees Fahrenheit, hot enough to melt lead.

Venus is not much closer to the sun than we are, but it absorbs massive amounts of heat, due to the presence of such a high amount of CO_2. Venus has a "runaway greenhouse effect," according to scientists. So we know, based on observation, that too little CO_2 would make the planet cold and inhospitable, like Mars (-20 degrees); and too much CO_2 would make the planet hot and uninhabitable, like Venus.

Earth will not likely become Venus, regardless of what we do. No one is suggesting that. What we are worried about, though, is much more likely. Small, but significant disruption of the Earth's self-regulating CO_2 cycle would have a substantial impact on life and civilization. Slight average temperature variations of only a few degrees Celsius would be enough to cause calamitous consequences. Oceans would rise, wiping out cities and civilizations that occupy oceanfront real estate. Melting polar ice caps, combined with too much CO_2 in the oceans, would alter the chemistry of the oceans, causing mass extinctions of sea life. Higher temperatures and

215

changing oceans also contribute to extreme weather events, such as massive hurricanes, tornadoes, blizzards (yes, even blizzards can be caused by global warming), droughts and other events.

We are already seeing many of these consequences, just as they were predicted in the 1980s and 1990s. First and foremost, we have seen the average global temperature increase at an alarming rate since the 1960s. The ten hottest years ever recorded have all taken place since 1998. 2014 was the hottest year ever recorded, and then 2015 was. And then 2016 was. While 2017 and 2018 have been *slightly* cooler than 2016, it was still way above average, and the overall trend is expected to continue to rise.

We have also seen rising temperatures in the oceans. The oceans absorb more heat from the sun, and this has a major impact on weather patterns and marine life. The increase in carbon dioxide in the oceans is also causing acidification, which also impacts marine life. And rising sea levels have already been observed. In the past century, average sea levels have risen over 7 inches, and the rate is accelerating.

We are also seeing the polar ice caps and glaciers around the world melting at a rapid pace. In fact, the ice is melting at a higher rate than scientists initially predicted. Since 1966, reduction of snow cover has reached 10%, and it, too, is accelerating. Some scientists have estimated that the Arctic could be completely ice-free within the next decade.

This is what we are faced with. The climate of the world is changing dramatically, and scientists agree that humans are causing, or at least greatly contributing to it. Almost all scientists that have studied climate change agree that the production of carbon emissions by humans is causing the planet to warm.

Despite this bleak outlook, it has proven futile to convince some of our nation's leaders that action needs to be taken to reduce our carbon output. The scientists have said that if we don't stop producing so much CO2, we are going to die, but there is an unyielding opposition to any legislation aimed at reducing carbon emissions. They call themselves 'climate skeptics,' but, as pointed out by a famous Science Guy, they should be called 'climate change deniers.' Skepticism suggests that there is some honest debate, and the climate scientists agree that there is no debate – anthropogenic global warming is occurring, and it will have dire consequences.

Climate change deniers either claim that climate change isn't happening, or that it is happening, but humans aren't responsible, or we don't have enough information one way or the other. Some cling to the notion that the climate is always changing, and that the Earth is simply going through a natural cycle, and the impact of human activity is inconsequential. And sometimes, when it snows in winter, some Republican Congressperson will bring a snow ball into the Senate chamber to prove that global warming is a hoax. That's right, some of these people believe - or claim to believe - that the entire scientific community is participating in a grand conspiracy to scare everyone into giving them grant money to combat climate change. In fact, in Louisiana, State Representative Lenar Whitney referred to climate change as "the greatest deception in the history of mankind."

It is absolutely undisputed that the scientific community overwhelmingly supports the idea of anthropogenic climate change. Of course, as the climate deniers point out so readily, consensus doesn't necessarily mean they are right.

The tired old analogy they use is the classic Copernican debate. Back in the 16th century, the "scientific" community believed that the earth was the center of the universe – the so-called "geo-centric" theory. One man, Copernicus, went against the scientific consensus and said that the earth circled the sun- the highly controversial "helio-centric" theory. He was branded a heretic, and suffered many negative repercussions as a result of challenging the prevailing knowledge of the time. Turns out, the consensus was wrong, and the geo-centrist denier, Copernicus, was right. Therefore, the climate deniers must be right, too, right?

What the climate skeptics fail to realize is that there really was no such thing as scientific consensus at the time. In fact, modern scientific method was not developed until the 18th century, and not widely in use until the 19th century. The geo-centric theory was therefore only the prevailing theory because the Church said so. In order to comply with sacred scripture, the Earth had to be the center of the universe. This theory could then be supported by explaining the movement of the night sky with selective understanding. In other words, the "scientists" of the time started with the conclusion that the Earth was center, and then interpreted the evidence to fit that conclusion. That was not good science (obviously) and it cannot be compared to scientific consensus as it exists today.

Now, let's talk about the consensus that exists today. The scientific consensus vis-a-vis climate change is that (1) the Earth is getting warmer, (2) the warming is mostly due to human activity, and (3) If greenhouse gas emission continue, the warming will accelerate. Studies by reputable organizations find that approximately 97% of climate scientists agree with the consensus. In one study, 97% of "actively publishing" climate scientists were convinced that the consensus is correct. Interestingly, of those few that were unconvinced had significantly fewer publication than those that were convinced, indicating that the "unconvinced" had done less research..

Despite these numbers, conservatives still insist that the matter is not settled, and not surprisingly, almost 50% of average citizens don't believe in climate change. They want to base policy going forward, and take a 'do-nothing' approach to climate change, based on the (biased?) opinion of a few fringe scientists. And while we're talking about (biased?) scientists, it is interesting to note that a few of the more visible ones have some interesting relationships with certain moneyed interests.

See, when all the scientists, doctors, researchers, etc. agree on an issue - such as climate change - and that issue stands to harm some special interest's special interests, those special interests will resort to making up their own, verifiable facts to refute the scientific consensus. The only way to do that, is to find scientists that agree with them – or who *will* agree with them, for the right price.

Naomi Oreskes and Erik Conway wrote a book about this phenomenon, titled <u>Merchants of Doubt</u>. Oreskes and Conway write that a handful of politically conservative scientists, with strong ties to particular industries, have "played a disproportionate role in debates about controversial questions". The authors write that this has resulted in "deliberate obfuscation" of the issues which has had an influence on public opinion and policy-making.

The book criticizes the so-called "Merchants of Doubt," some predominantly American science key players, including, specifically, Bill Nierenberg, Fred Seitz, and Fred Singer. These three physicists have been active on important issues such as acid rain, tobacco smoking, global warming and pesticides. Oreskes and Conway claim that these scientists have challenged and diluted the scientific consensus in the various fields, as of the dangers of smoking, the effects of acid rain, the existence of the ozone hole, and most recently, the existence of anthropogenic climate change.

They point out that Seitz and Singer helped to form institutions such as the Heritage Foundation, Competitive Enterprise Institute and Marshall Institute in the United States. Funded by corporations and conservative foundations, these right-wing organizations have opposed many forms of state intervention or regulation of U.S. citizens. The book lists similar tactics in each case: "discredit the science, disseminate false information, spread confusion, and promote doubt".

The Merchants of Doubt also questions the ability of the media to differentiate between false truth and the actual science in question. In fact, the journalistic norm of 'balanced reporting' has helped, according to the authors, to *amplify* the misleading messages of the contrarians. Oreskes and Conway state: "small numbers of people can have large, negative impacts, especially if they are organized, determined and have access to power".

The work of Oreskes and Conway builds on the work of previous scholars that noticed the same thing. One historian, in particular, is Robert Proctor, a Professor of History at Stanford University, who proposed the idea of agnotology, or the study of culturally induced ignorance or doubt, particularly the publication of inaccurate or misleading scientific data. Proctor first coined the term in his 1995 book, <u>The Cancer Wars: How Politics Shapes What We Know and Don't Know About Cancer</u>. He stated that "[h]istorians and philosophers of science have tended to treat ignorance as an ever-expanding vacuum into which knowledge is sucked... [Ignorance] has a distinct and changing political geography that is often an excellent indicator of the politics of knowledge. We need a political agnotology to complement our political epistemologies."

Just as Oreskes and Conway did in Merchants, Proctor cited the tobacco industry's conspiracy to manufacture doubt about the cancer risks of tobacco use. Under the banner of science, the industry produced research about everything except tobacco hazards to exploit public uncertainty. He cites as other causes of culturally induced ignorance media neglect, corporate or governmental secrecy and suppression, document destruction, inattention, and forgetfulness.

Basically, this cabal of biased scientists gives its donors enough junk science to keep the debate alive. Talking points that raise just enough doubt to fit the narrative that they, themselves, have constructed, that "the science is not settled." But, the science *is* settled. Climate change is not just *going* to be catastrophic, climate change is an *ongoing* catastrophe. By allowing this small group of professional contrarians to fill the air waves with pseudo-science and vague rebuttals, the mainstream media has abetted the miseducation of 50% of the American population concerning a very real and existential crisis. The control of Congress and the White House by carbon-friendly sycophants has made the crisis even more dire. Hopefully there is still time to vote-in climate change policy, but we need to ensure that our candidates are dedicated to that goal above all else. must remember, one day soon, it *will* be too late.

XXVI.
Climate Change:
A Gateway to Armageddon?

Regardless of which of these categories the climate change skeptics fall into, the result is the same. They all want to do nothing to change our fossil fuel-dependent lifestyle. Even though the continued existence of mankind is potentially at stake, they refuse to take action. The question is - why?

Well, the most obvious reason "skeptics" continue to "hear no evil" is pure, unabashed greed. Nearly all vocal deniers share one thing in common - they are all vested in, bought off and/or paid for by companies that are in the business of producing, refining, or greatly relying on fossil fuels. Oil and gas companies, coal companies, energy companies, companies with large power-hungry factories - these are the interests that will be most severely affected by reduced carbon emissions, and they spend many millions of dollars buying scientists and government officials to combat the scientific consensus. And they have run a largely successful disinformation campaign that has many millions of people convinced that climate change is scientific fakery.

But there is another reason that certain people continue to deny any change in global climate linked to human activity - religion. The thought occurred to me recently when I was reading the comment thread on some article about some weather anomaly that killed a lot of people. One commenter stated that all these catastrophic weather events that we've seen in recent years are evidence that God is punishing us humans for our sins - you know, abortion, gay marriage, all those things that seem to make conservative skin crawl. A little research led me quickly to deduce that religion does, indeed, play an important role in the continued denial of climate change. Just last week Anne Graham Lotz, daughter of famed evangelist Billy Graham, made headlines claiming that recent trends in LGBT rights have caused God to turn away from us, suggesting that if we turn to Him He will protect us from those violent weather patterns linked to global warming.

Of course, not all religious people are climate deniers. In fact, many religious organizations are enthusiastic supporters of climate science, as they see humans' role as "stewards" of the Earth charged with the protection of the environment. Pro-environmental Christians believe that depleting the Earth's resources or degrading the environment is "an offense to God." One particularly influential environmental religious voice is that of Sir John Houghton, a former professor of atmospheric physics at Oxford. Houghton actually played an integral role in the development of the Intergovernmental Panel on Climate Change (IPCC), and is seen as one of the foremost experts in the area of climate change.

But there is another faction of the religious right, especially here in America, that insists that climate change is "un-Biblical," and therefore cannot be a real threat. For instance, right-wing conservative politician, Rick Santorum, once publicly stated:

"We were put on this Earth as creatures of God to have dominion over the Earth . . . for our benefit not for the Earth's benefit."

It turns out that the link between religiosity and climate change denial has been empirically demonstrated. Surveys show that while 80% of non-religious people in America believe in climate change, only 56% of highly religious people do. These deniers tend to think that since God created the Earth, humans are powerless to disrupt the balance put in place by the Almighty. They suggest that the scriptures, specifically Genesis 1:26-28 cited by Mr. Santorum above, gave dominion of the Earth to humans, and that we can do whatever we want with it without consequence.

There is also another way religion impedes global efforts to counteract climate change. Many Americans, more than you might think, have little or no desire to avert global catastrophe. Evangelical Christians that believe in the "Second Coming" of Jesus Christ fall into this category. While some of these evangelicals may actually believe that climate change is real, they are not interested in fixing it. To them, the end of civilization, or the Biblical "end times," would signal the Second Coming, and would therefore be *a good thing*. David Barker and David Pearce demonstrated this in an article published in the journal <u>Political Research Quarterly</u> where they showed:

"A belief in the Second Coming reduces the probability of strongly agreeing that the government should take action [to curb climate change] by more than 12 percent. In a corresponding manner, a belief in the Second Coming increases the probability of disagreeing with government action to curb global warming by more than 10 percent."

This is truly frightening to me. The thought that there are people, some in positions of power and authority, including some well-known Congressmen, that have no desire to thwart a pending apocalypse. These same people have no fear of nuclear war, viral plagues, or any other calamity, because it would mean that their savior is coming to save them. To them, even if climate change is real, it is not a crisis, but a gift from God. All the science in the world won't change their minds, because we not only have to convince them that climate change is real, but that their holy book is wrong - or at least that their strained interpretation of their holy book is wrong. Either way, changing someone's religion is much harder than changing someone's mind.

It is clear that religion has a negative impact on ongoing efforts to reduce carbon emissions and protect against the devastating effects of climate change. Luckily, there are large religious organizations, including the Catholic church, that are on the side of climate scientists. Hopefully, with continued education, we will be able to convince enough of the climate deniers to join in the fight for clean, renewable energy. Hopefully, even the highly religious can be converted to this cause, and we can postpone Armageddon for a bit longer.

<u>AFTERWORD</u>

Francois Lemoyne's final masterpiece, entitled 'Time Saving Truth from Falsehood and Envy,' featured on the cover of this book, is an allegory that couldn't be more fitting. Lemoyne captured the spirit of the struggle that has been waging for all of human history. Falsehood and Envy are constantly trying to destroy Truth, but eventually, Time will come to the rescue. All the articles and essays contained herein have been an attempt to shed light on areas of public policy that affect the lives of all Americans, and on which cable news and talk radio ceaselessly attempt to mislead or downright lie. But we do not have to listen. We have the ability to do something about it. And it starts with the desire to know – to fact check our politicians, pundits and preachers. And that is what I am constantly at work doing- trying to stay ahead of the propaganda, and everyone who is interested in truth should be doing likewise.

This is the 21st century. We've been to the moon. We have hybrid cars, and cellular telephones with more computing power than Apollo 11. But most importantly, we have instant access to information. There is a reason this is called the Information Age. The internet, while admittedly filled with pornography, conspiracy theories and computer viruses, is also filled with information – on virtually every topic imaginable. If I want to know where the best ice-fishing in northern Michigan is, I only need to

Google it and I get 4,170,000 hits. Not all will lead me to ice-fishing nirvana, but I'll bet if I spent a little time reading through a few of the more legitimate-looking articles, I will find a pretty good spot to build my shack.

I grew up in the 1980's, before the advent of the internet, when personal computers did little more than play 8-bit arcade games. If we wanted to find answers, we had to rely on libraries and card catalogues, dictionaries and encyclopedias. It took effort, and time to do research, and find answers to complicated questions.

And quite often, when we did take the time to do research, the information we received was conspicuously outdated, long before we undertook the endeavor. Cutting edge information is well-preserved in bound volumes, but the speed it travels in this medium is dismal. Even with newspapers that publish everyday, by the time you are reading it, it is yesterday's news.

But now, we have the internet. It contains all those libraries and encyclopedias, but it also contains billions of other sources of information, always up to date and instantly transmitted, all at the touch of a button. No secret is safe. No question unanswered. And you can access that vast universe of information from anywhere, on your laptop computer, tablet or cell phone. You can look up answers while you're sitting in your doctor's waiting room, or while waiting your turn at the DMV. You can browse virtually all the acquired knowledge of human civilization, while you're sitting in your bathtub.

The point is, we don't have to listen to politicians and partisan pundits anymore. We don't have to take their word for anything. We can search for the answers ourselves, from practically anywhere. And with smart search engines, finding answers to most common questions is relatively easy.

However, an important caveat is that the articles you find on the internet, whether they be from Fox News or John Smith's Opinion.com, will often have a biased point of view. Some news sources are liberal (MSNBC, Huffington Post) and some are more conservative (any Fox News affiliate, Rush Limbaugh). I strongly encourage you to go to more than one source.

The truth is out there, folks, and it is almost certainly at our fingertips at any time of the day. Little, invisible fragments of information, floating through the air, waiting to be captured, assembled, and analyzed. The answers to every question, just a few clicks of a mouse away. We don't have to rely on the milkman (do those still exist?) to tell us how important calcium is. A single Google search for "calcium importance" returns 9,380,000 links.

And that's really what biased reporting and editorial – I'll admit, even the articles in this book - is all about. It is a sales pitch by someone, or some group, with an agenda. They want to sell you their product - usually in the form of their favorite hate. True, the more partisan sales pitches are focused more on pre-existing customers, but there is always the possibility, or danger, that an undecided voter will be influenced by some particularly erudite and charming pundit that disingenuously camouflages biased opinion as accepted fact. That is where I draw the line with this book.

I have presented my side of the story. And now the gauntlet has been laid down. Go forth, all ye multitudes of devoted followers, and challenge my side of the story. If you agree with all I've said, do nothing, and be happy and content in knowing I have not led you astray. But for all you naysayers, please, go prove me wrong. The important thing is that you become engaged, one way or another.

-J. Thomas Beasley

<u>About the Author</u>

Jesse Thomas Beasley was born and raised in Savannah, Georgia. He graduated from Armstrong State University with a Bachelor of Arts in Political Science and Public Administration before moving to New Orleans, Louisiana with his wife, Happy to attend law school. Jesse graduated from Loyola University School of Law in 2004 and has been practicing law in New Orleans ever since, where he lives with his wife and three children. Jesse's law practice focuses on public interest advocacy, including representing indigent clients in both civil and criminal proceedings, often on a pro bono basis.

www.ingramcontent.com/pod-product-compliance
Lightning Source LLC
Chambersburg PA
CBHW051439250726
48655CB00001B/135